The Land of Silent Morning

AQUARIUS PRESS

Detroit, Michigan

The Land of Silent Morning by Kateleen K. Washington

Edited by Sharon Stanford, Cathryn Williams and Sylvia McClain

Names, characters, places and incidents are products of the author's recollection, and all American names have been changed.

Copyright © 2009 by Kateleen K. Washington

Aquarius Press
PO Box 23096
Detroit, MI 48223
(313) 515-8122
www.aquariuspressbookseller.net

ISBN 978-0-9819208-9-4
Cover art by Aquarius Press
Library of Congress Control Number 2009922834

Printed in the United States of America

Dedication

This book is dedicated to all who helped me with the writing of this book over these past 10 years. Special thanks to Sylvia McClain for her encouragement.

Preface

Along the journey through my past, there were too many unresolved emotional issues in my life. Whether I was consciously realizing it or not, those issues had been stacking up in my heart throughout my life since I was seven years old. I felt that life had chosen me instead of me choosing life. I did not know what the reason was, nor why I was born on this earth, but surely I did not choose the life I had. I lived in the opposite of the light and I had to deal with excruciating pain in my heart all alone. My heart had been torn and shredded into a thousand pieces; yet, I continued to live without support. I endured hell for many decades, because I could not unlock the mystery of my life. I was eager to find out who I was, and sometime ago, I searched for an answer. Since then, I haven't known how to stop searching. It has taken me 48 years to find out who I truly am.

In 1996, I began to discover who this person called "Kay" really is. The only way I could understand was through a spiritual awakening that assisted me in the present and guided me to my past. I never imagined I would have to relive my Korean past again in the United States. The circumstances were different and the times were dreadful, filled with anxiety and anguish. I spent ten long years searching to heal wounds. Now I have become much stronger and I understand my past much better. I have put things in perspective. The completed puzzle was put together piece-by-piece and I survived. I have finally let go of my past; I am able to hug my other being and I have become my own hero.

As I leave my past behind, I am able to speak to my mom through the silence of time. Mom, thank you. *Will you forgive me?* Yes, I forgive you. I love you and I miss you very much. You brought me into the world so that I could experience life. If it wasn't for you, how could I be in this wonderful place? I did not think in my wildest dreams that I would be where I am today. I am a human angel. I will be walking through the journey of my life, dedicating my heart to the people who need emotional support. I will gladly stretch out my arms to those who need hugs so that their hearts can be healed. I will give 100 percent to those who want my love and guidance.

All people come here to learn, and that is through life experience. We must learn and not repeat the same mistakes. I truly feel that most people want to forget about the past, but the past makes us who we are in the present. The only way we can avoid making the same mistakes is to be kind to ourselves and share kindness with our fellow human beings. In my heart I will always thank those who have given their time for me to succeed. You are awesome friends, and I love you all. My blessings go out to you, and I pray for safe journeys in your lives.

One

The summer night sky was crystal clear, and the golden brilliance of the moonlight shone over the small, quiet village. The twinkling stars were lined up like the formation of an army squad standing over the treetops. These trees had grown over the quiet village above the rooftops and they were the only things that witnessed what happened to the little girl that night. Little girl eyes were fixed on the gigantic tree trunks and their limbs. The girl sensed that there was something always watching her over from the treetops. As the wind gently lifted up its limbs of the tree, the little girl danced with it. She had no one else in the world. She had to trust herself and the trees began whispering to her, "We will protect you. The only thing you have to do is just let it be." She still remembers the night so vividly. A vulnerable little girl who was not aware of what kind of evil was waiting with unspeakable surprises that cool summer night. She would not know that her life was going to be shaped by one tormented moment that would cause intense suffering the rest of her life. In fact, no one ever knew who she was, not even herself. Now, she is standing in front of a mirror and sees the reflection of her other self clearly: who she was and who she has become.

In the silence of the savage night, sometimes I hear myself as the little girl crying in the darkness, hoping that someone would rescue her in time. An innocent little girl who stood in the darkness for many years filled with devastation, fears and horrors. The horrors that made me grow up fast without even having time to blossom throughout my childhood. I was too young to realize that future happenings would have an impact on the rest of my life.

I remember living in a beautiful house. The house was located in a suburban area in Seoul, Korea called Young San. It had many rooms with wooden floors, a tiled-roof and a huge courtyard. In the courtyard there was a beautiful baby. The baby had an adorable bright smile with cute, chubby cheeks. Uncommonly, the baby had huge, deep, dark brown eyes that lit up all the neighbors. I was well accepted by my parents and loved by everyone the day I was born.

One summer afternoon, I was wearing a diaper and playing by the well. My mother was washing the clothes on the washing board and glanced at me frequently with her usual smile. For hours I sat in the mud and ate it, plastering it all over my whole body. I knew how to amuse myself. I was an infant who took a very short nap, woke up, and quietly played with my dirty diaper in the room alone. I was different, peculiar maybe, an abnormal baby as my mom told me when I was older. She told me that when I was growing up I hardly ever cried and was the quietest infant of all five of her children.

Several years passed. I could hear the sound of music flowing from a record player; it was a waltz. My dad asked me to dance with him. He was standing patiently in a huge room with his face filled with joy. I ran up to him quickly, like a duck. He opened his arms to catch me. He held my little hands softly and my response was to put my two feet on top of his. As the waltz played, he spun me wildly through the huge room several times. I saw my mother sitting at the edge of the room watching with a joyous grin on her face.

Unfortunately, all my life, I only have a few unforgettable memories of my father. I have very distinct images of him. I remember deep dark brown eyes like mine, dark hair, and a slim build. He always looked immaculate even though he stayed home a lot.

I recall the events that were so harsh that I had to block them out from my memories because now I am experiencing sudden flashbacks of my home and my family. My family consisted of Mom, Dad and eventually four sisters with me being the oldest. My family was very poor. I mean dirt poor. I cannot remember Mom or Dad ever having a job but I remember them going to the garbage dump to gather empty cans, bottles, and paper to get money from a recycling center in order to buy food.

Sometimes my grandmother helped them financially. She had two daughters, my mother and her sister, who was my aunt. My grandmother's two daughters were born in North Korea and emigrated to South Korea during the Korean War. Sadly, I never knew my grandfather in person, but I've seen his picture. My grandfather had been killed by Communists because of his social status. My grandmother was a strong-willed woman who had raised both daughters by herself, which was unheard of during that period. In fact, she had sent both daughters to the best high school in Seoul, Korea. My grandmother was a rich woman who owned a high class business on Jeju-do Island, which was about 1,500 miles from Seoul. When she visited my family, we would not be hungry for months. However, my grandmother really favored her older daughter over my mother. She had married an affluent man who owned a theater and then worked in an executive position in downtown Seoul, according to my mom. They had two boys and a girl, and an older adopted daughter who committed suicide when she reached her teenage years.

On the other hand, my mom and dad were treated unequally by my grandmother. When my mom met my dad, she was in high school. My dad was in college in Japan, according to my dad's family. He had his Korean sweetheart who had worked at the American Army Base before he met my mom. His girlfriend had a son with my dad who was three years older than me, whom I eventually met when I was in my 20's. When I met him, he was with his mother, and I was with my mother, in an orchard somewhere in Seoul. I took time to study him, and he too, had dark deep brown eyes filled with

9

sadness. Like my father's eyes. He knew where his father was, but he could not dare to hear his voice or see his face. To my knowledge, in Korean culture my stepbrother was a bastard and he could not ever be accepted as a son. Unfortunately, he never met his dad when he was alive. My dad left his son with a grudge which smoldered in his heart forever. Sometimes though, I still wonder about how he feels, not knowing my dad all his life.

Obviously, there was a reason my grandmother did not welcome my dad with open arms. He already had a girlfriend with a son; he wasn't someone who had given her a good first impression and he was fortuneless. Grandmother predicted that he was not a man who would take care of or be responsible for his family. He may have been a nice, intelligent, well-educated man full of book knowledge, but he did not have common sense and neither did my mother. My mother was jealous and envious of what my dad had. She wanted to have him and keep him in her own fenced fantasy world and she succeeded. Eventually, she got pregnant with me and this is how she brought my dad into her life, without marrying my father. My grandmother never approved of either of them being together. Nevertheless, their lives had begun miserably filled with hostility.

I was about five years old and I wasn't the baby I used to be. I was standing in front of the house that looked like an Indian teepee, except that my home was underground. The house was a dug out, a hole about five or six feet deep, approximately seven feet wide with a black tar roof. There was a ladder against the dirt wall in order to get in and out of the home. Of course, there wasn't a wooden door like a modern home; instead, a straw mat hung in front of the ladder. The floor was made out of a straw mat that reminded me of a barn. Thus, it stayed a little warm even in winter and cool in summer.

As my family was poverty-stricken, we eventually had a total of seven in our family which lived in the one room. I played with my first sister who was about three years old. We never had dolls or toys to play with. Our play object was dirt instead of dolls or toys. Although every once in a while, mom gave us steamed sweet potatoes while we were playing. That was the most delicious and sweetest taste ever. It was almost like sucking candies. Despite how destitute we were, as long as we ate barley with soy sauce that was good enough and it was a feast. However, I cannot remember seeing my dad in this home at all. Maybe he wasn't living with my mom then. Whatever the reason, in my memory, my dad was absent until my twin sisters were born in a white brick house. It was a gorgeous white brick house. It stood in front of the Han River which my grandmother bought for us. In this house I was constantly working around the home. The house was big and it had a kitchen and doors.

Time passed and I started first grade. My dad was home and I saw him all the time. We were happy, but I never heard laughing in my family. At this time, life got a little a better for our family financially. Nevertheless, that was the time when arguments arose day after day and hardly ever stopped. In spite of their arguments, I did not fear them, but I was always mindful around them. No matter what happened, I did not want any part of it. After a year might have passed, I was still in the first grade. I cannot remember any fun in class or any schoolmates. Maybe there was nothing worth remembering. Sometimes though, I wish I could remember something good when I was in the classroom, but I cannot. I was ready for the second grade when my fifth baby sister was born. As soon as the baby arrived, our lives became tougher because with twins, and there were three babies in our home. My mom and dad had physical fights from this time on. There were savage beatings, yelling, and thrashing around each other when they fought. It seemed like they were trying to kill each other every day, yet, their hateful marriage continued. Our traditional culture kept them together without divorce or separation.

I remember the horrible fights and how mom usually started to nag him about life in general. The most important issues were food on the table, money, and so forth. My dad listened quietly without a word. Finally she pushed him to the edge. He was not a loud man at all but all of a sudden I heard his voice going through the roof. At last, mom had pushed him over the top and she endangered her life. Everything could have been prevented if she had been quiet for a moment. In a split second, his unstoppable rage overcame him, swallowed his usual quiet nature and it turned him into a vicious, angry being. He became a haughtily offensive character whose ego had been bruised in order to defend himself. His intense violence began very quietly. He said to Mom, "Drop it," but she wouldn't stop and it continued. The obscene words were said by both of them and the outburst woke up the neighbors. I still think that if Mom had been quiet for a moment, or if she had the wisdom to deal with situations wisely, he would never have hurt her at all.

It was 1963, early afternoon during a winter blizzard. My parents had an intense argument which led to another physical fight. I was usually not around during their fights but this one particular day, I was in the room. The room had a few blankets that were neatly folded in the corner of the room, and my sisters were sleeping by the charcoal stove because it was warm. Mom was making us dinner and glanced at my sleeping baby sisters. Usually in winter, we ate earlier than usual and all activities were ended by dinner time. Mom said something to Dad. I don't know what she said, but in a split second, the wood cutting board was flying over her head. The cutting board had been by the stove and he hit her on the head with it. The top of her head was split open. Streams of blood flowed down her forehead. I felt threatened by Dad's action for the first time. I couldn't breathe from all the crying. I handed her a towel, hoping that the bleeding would stop. As she held the towel down on the wound, she asked me to fetch her traditional Korean dress. I brought her an orange colored folk dress. While she put on her dress, I tried to hold the towel on her bleeding head. It was the first time I saw blood and I was scared. Finally, she had decided to leave all of us. She realized she could no longer bear her sufferings. She made the choice because she felt there was no hope. She went out the door full of tears in her eyes and up to the dike behind our home. I followed her as long as I could in the blizzard. I was screaming for her. "Mom, don't go." By the time I got to the bridge, the bus was stopped. "Mom, please don't go." I begged. I hung on to her dress with all my strength. We both cried. Mysteriously, I still cannot remember whether or not she really left home that day or just went to her sister's. The only memory I had was of the bridge.

The second huge fight was during a dreadful summer, right after the monsoon season in July through August in 1964. I saw the floods had washed away all the crops and house goods were floating down the river. We lost some of our crops because of this disaster too. We used to have some land down the hill. We planted vegetables; corn, barley and a few types of fruit plants. It seemed our luck had turned bad again. Mom was nagging Dad about something. I was in the kitchen sitting quietly near the stove. Suddenly, the door flung open. My dad burst into the kitchen. He took the gasoline can into the room and poured gasoline over everything in it. He came back into the kitchen once more, grabbing the burning wood from the stove. I yelled very loud. "Dad, stop!" I screamed much louder hoping that the neighbors would hear me. A few neighbors ran over to our home. They held down my dad and said, "You cannot hurt them, Mr. Choe." Our neighbors were talking about my sisters. They held down my dad for a long time. At last, he calmed down and dropped the burning wood from his hand. He looked at me helplessly. As he turned his face away from me and wiped his tears, I witnessed his tears. He was not a monster. That day, he almost killed us and our home could have gone up in flames. I was still standing in the kitchen by the door, holding his arms tightly without a word. The horror had ended with my tears and screams.

After that fight, my parents didn't talk to each other for a while. However, I became numb. I could not express my feelings to anyone or talk because I didn't have a friend, not even at school. No one

13

ever got close to me and I was always alone. I had never spoken about my family or problems within the family to anyone. I buried all my emotions deep in my heart. I became even more distant from everyone around me. I shut myself off from the world. As a little girl, my personality was traumatized by too many bad memories of my parents, and yet, there are a few good memories I have of my dad. On several occasions, he loved to give me piggyback rides when I came home from school.

My school was in the metropolitan area of Seoul, but it hadn't been developed. Our home was in the middle of two rivers. One was behind our home, Han River. When I went to the school, the boat docked at the front of our home near the farm. The boat then dropped me near the school. I walked to the farmland and up to the dike about a half-mile to the class. It was at the end of first grade, making it around 1963 or 1964. I still remember the day distinctly. In the class, the teacher was handing out certificates and perfect attendance. The teacher announced my name and said, "Kyong Mi, you have perfect attendance." Schoolmates were clapping and I bowed my head. I was done with first grade and happy. I was filled with excitement.

Being filled with excitement got me huge trouble. I wasn't paying attention to where I was going after school, and I ended up getting lost. That afternoon I was walking instead of hopping on the boat. It was getting dark and the sun was setting west. I saw the burning color of the sun, but it had a dark tint to it. I was scared and alone. I dropped my book bag and cried. I looked around to see if there was anyone coming my way. As I looked around I saw a man walking toward me. As he got closer, I saw it was my father. I was thrilled to see him. He was my hero. I ran to him with my arms wide open. I was that little girl like the duck when we were dancing the waltz. He picked me up and put me on his shoulders and carried me all the way home.

In October of the same year, we received a telegram. My mother said that my uncle wanted to visit my dad. I had never met my uncle before, nor had I ever heard of my uncle. I did not know my dad had family. My dad read to us what uncle had written. My uncle wanted our family to move closer to him. After a few months of thinking it over (during which time I did not return to school) my parents decided to move closer to my dad's family in Ulsan. It was about 198 miles south of Seoul on the South Coast.

Very quickly, we sold everything that we owned. It wasn't much, but it gave us enough money to make the trip to Ulsan. On the way we had to stay in a hotel by the Seoul Train Station. All seven of us had a chance to explore the city briefly. I had never seen the city of Seoul before. The city was adding buildings everywhere. The train station was fixing its structure which had been damaged. Maybe, it had been damaged from the Korean War, or it was just old. It had a long history of many patriots who died. People were also still rebuilding their lives in the city as well. From the station, I could see the Nam San Park cable car. I remember that there was a construction site behind the train station. I looked around. I saw a giant mountain of sand where I played wildly. I had great fun. I ran down from the top of the sand. I giggled with my sister. It was the only time our family had happiness being together. I was only eight years old and loved every second of this adventure.

We took three to four days to get south to my uncle's place. On the train, I saw many parts of the different cities. It was beautifully designed by the nature. The train crossed the many bridges over the rivers. There was the ocean, white sand and scorching heat. When we finally arrived it was night. Everyone was very pleased to see us. My dad had a large family and they had been waiting for us to arrive. What a wonderful feeling I had. It was all a new experience and I was bashful. It was like seeing someone other than my immediate family. To me, they were an upper class family. In addition, their customs were different than ours. My uncle was the Chief of Police in the city. My cousins were all grown men and were very nice to my sisters and me.

After weeks passed, uncle and his wife were looking for a place for our family to settle down. At the same time, my mom and dad were finding a school so that my sister and I could continue our education. My uncle found a home, a home owned by an older woman. She lived alone, next our new place. It was two separate houses but joined by one foundation of the ceiling. He rented a home for us on the hill. He paid the total our expenses; education, food, and roof over our head. Our new home was less than a thousand square feet. It had one bedroom and kitchen. It was a mixture of mud and straw. It dried like brick and was used for the walls. The foundation of the ceiling was wood. The roof was black tar used in first layer for the rain, and the second layers were straws. From the outside it looked like two huts; maybe it was the way of traditional living in south.

Along the hill, the gigantic cotton trees were standing proudly welcoming our family. As we got to the top of the hill, we could see the whole village. Straight ahead from where we were standing, we saw our home alone. There was nothing else nearby except a tall grown wheat farm. Our family finally got settled. My sister and I started school. The fun started for me in the class. I was popular with classmates because I was from a different place and I spoke a different dialect. They loved me and adored me. I skipped the second grade and went to third grade. My sister was in kindergarten. I was a very bright, intelligent and happy little girl, even though I had been through terrible times with my parents. At the same time my dad had found better health and I was able to walk with him some evenings. Every time when he walked with me, I noticed that his lips changed to a purple color. He had to rest anywhere along the dirt road. I asked my dad, "Are you sick?" and he would say, "No, I just need a little rest." I had such a curiosity about my dad's condition to my mom. But I couldn't. I was not allowed to ask about adult problems. It was Korean custom.

There was one elementary teacher who was amazed by everything I did in class. I got good grades in every subject. The teacher encouraged me to join the marching band. I played the harmonica well and ended up in holiday parades in the town. I was wearing green shorts with white stockings, a white shirt with a green vest; eventually, I was wearing a matching green hat. Sometimes, I pictured the face of this teacher. How wonderful she was to me. She was tall, with curly hair and an unusually light complexion. She was a gorgeous, compassionate, and kind person.

Everything went smoothly for a while. My mom and dad did not fight and we always had good food. Also, there was someone always closer to our family, my dad's and our neighbors. One summer day, my mom took me swimming. The water was the color of the rainbow. Maybe it was the reflection of the sun in the crystal, sparking water. It was the famous Tae Wha River in Korea. I may compare it to the Mississippi River in the United States. The riverbed was carpeted in soft, white sand. The sun was warming the calm water and inviting me into the pool. My mom held my little hand. We waded in the river slowly for a while. She found a place where there was a water pool. How beautiful she was. She was as beautiful as the rainbow and the most gentle spirit on earth. She asked me to lie down on the palms of her hands. She glided me around the pool of calm water. It was the first time she showed me how to swim. I was a girl with so much potential and talents to do anything. We had enough fun for a day. There were many days for me to learn and practice swim lessons with Mom. Toward the sunset, we finally got out of the pool and headed home.

While I did well in school and was blessed, there was something terrible and ugly waiting for me on the horizon. One weekend during the summer, we visited my uncle's place. I met my oldest cousin, Sung Chan, my uncle's oldest son. He was very distinguished, charming and about thirty years old. He had just returned from Vietnam. Sung Chan's father proudly introduced him to our family. He had been an excellent soldier and a good son. He was just visiting his favorite uncle, my father. He wanted to meet his little cousins. He said, "You are Kyong Mi." I looked at him and I liked him right away. We chatted, laughed and I enjoyed his company. He was like an older brother I never had. My uncle had three boys and a girl and Sung Chan was the best one.

One night we got invited to my uncle's and it had gotten late, so my parents let me and my sisters stay for the night while they returned home. My uncle's sleeping arrangements were such that boys and girls slept in the same room. This was common Korean culture in the old days. My cousin, Sung Chan, carried my sisters in the room near the courtyard, by the front wooden gate. My sisters were sleeping soundly. I wasn't sleeping so he held my hand and came to the room. He left for where his father was, but he would come back to sleep in the same room with me and my sisters.

On the other hand, I could not sleep soundly like my sisters. I was always a light sleeper no matter where I was. I heard the sound of the opening door and I woke up. It was my cousin. He asked me to lie down beside him. He put his arm under my neck. It was deliciously comfortable and I soon fell asleep. He was different than my father. My father never held me like Sung Chan did. Suddenly I was awakening because I was very uncomfortable, and I felt that I wanted to urinate. When I opened my eyes, I was on top of his chest. I felt that something hard was touching my private area. Sung Chan's erection was rubbing against me. I tried pulling my body away from him, but I could not. I wanted to scream, but he was very forceful. He placed his one big hand over my mouth, and with his other big hand, he started fondling my vagina. He finally let go of me and I escaped outside.

I was free. I spent the rest of the night in the courtyard looking at the full moon. It was a big moon and had bright yellow color. The summer sky was clear, and I could see many stars. It was deadly peaceful and so quiet. It was so dark and quiet in the village and I was the one living on a dark planet. My eyes were fixed on a gigantic tree trunk and its limbs. After a time, I realized I was sitting on the ground, and I glanced at my body. I was wearing white pajamas and a sleeveless top. I did not know what was happening. I finally had the strength to look up at the sky again. The full moon was so high and bright, it was looking down on me like nothing had ever happened, but it had. An innocent, precious little girl was not so innocent anymore.

The next morning everyone got up early as usual and asked me how I slept. I told them I slept well and nodded in reinforcement. The reason I told them that was because I was ashamed. I knew that adults would rather not know about what went on. Besides, my parents never asked me about how I slept with my cousin either. After that night I learned to keep my mouth shut. I was becoming worse, not saying anything no matter what. I realized now that even though I didn't do anything wrong, I had always thought it was my fault. Not talking about it and keeping it to me was the only way I could protect myself from hurting. After the incident with Sung Chan, I only remember seeing him once more before my dad passed away. The only thing I remember about that encounter was Sung Chan walking up the hill toward my house. I ran back out of my house and hid. I heard the sound of my dad's voice through the back door.

That fall my dad passed away from tuberculosis. He was only 42 years old. I remember now how most of his life he had been ill. When he died, I was at school. Toward evening, my mom came to get me in the class. In the distance, I saw both my mom and my teacher were talking seriously. I knew then something went very wrong. Both of them were weeping, and soon my teacher called me and told me to go home with my mom. I don't remember if my mom told me about my dad's condition on the way home. When we came up the hill, I saw blue and white striped nightwear on a bamboo pole flying like a flag. I suppose this was some kind of tradition when

19

someone died. Everyone was moaning and sobbing, but for some reason I could not cry. I carried my baby sister on my back and stayed outside until the night fell.

The sun was setting down in the west. I remember leaning against a white brick wall. On the playground, I looked around, but no one was there. I was looking down the hill in the rice field. The rice field was plastered in cadmium yellow. It was fully grown and ready to harvest. It seemed to bow its head to the ground. I was taking in the information from the nature. Whether it was dark or light I was sucking in everything and keeping it in a safe place. At the time I really didn't understand about death. Maybe I was in shock and did not know what to think. I can't remember to this day why I was leaning against that white brick wall. Throughout that evening until the night, I was looking through the golden rice field aimlessly.

Three days later we held my father's funeral. The day of the morning sky was gray. Even the sky reflected my sadness and every once in a while there was thunder. It brought pouring rain at first, then sprinkled gently. It softened the ground. My mom was wearing a white cotton dress and a handmade straw-rope for a headpiece. I was carrying my baby sister on my back. Whether I realized it or not, I finally burst into tears. I saw my father's casket. The casket was made of wood, similarly, like pallet wood. In the old days the people used this wood to store vegetables and fruits. I was holding on to the casket and would not let go. I had finally understood that I would never see my beloved father again. Some people yanked me away from the casket rope. I was screaming for my dad. I saw my mom hold the casket and she could not stand up. There were many cousins, aunts, and uncles. Several young people lifted up the casket. Mom had to let go of my father. My aunts held her up. They followed behind the casket down the hill to the funeral bus. The bus was white and it drove my father and all of the relatives to the crematory. I was not allowed get on the bus. I watched until the last honor to my father was complete, and it was still raining. The day of my father's funeral, my happiness was also over. Tears I shed, it had turned to ice and it sank deep in my heart.

My mom did not notice how I was dealing with the death of my dad. She may not have been concerned about it at all. Her primary concern was how she would survive with five children and no job skills. A few months later the rest of my family returned to Seoul where my grandmother and aunt lived. The first thing my grandmother did for us was rent a house so that we could live close to her. When we arrived in Seoul, it was a dry and cold winter day. I felt that the weather was much colder. I was thinking back on how we had left Seoul with my dad and now came back without him. I hid my sadness deep within my ten-year-old soul. I pictured my father's generous smile, invitations of his deep dark eyes. He was reaching out his arms to hold me and dance around the room. At that moment, I felt emptiness inside me all over again endlessly, and wished he was with me.

Two

Within a month, after my father's death, we returned to Seoul where my grandmother and my aunt let us live with them for a short time. Their home was on a hill in a large wealthy community. The community we were in was a mixture of rich and poor getting along with each other and people were friendly and helpful in a way I didn't experience when my dad was alive. Soon, my grandmother found a rented house for my mother, my sisters and me. She was supporting us financially once more because mom did not have a job and also she could look out her front door on the hill and spy on us in our home. In front of our house, there was a community well where everyone got their water and socialized with each other. One of my new responsibilities was to get water for our home, but I also made money for us by lugging huge metal canisters on a coolie rack up the hill for customers.

Our rental house was a one bedroom with a kitchen and an outhouse. The bedroom was a raised heated cement platform and everyone had their own quilted mattress which lay directly on the floor. Everyone had to roll out their mattresses at night and roll it up each morning. The kitchen was a step down from the door and had a dirt floor. The countertop was built with brick and cement. Then under the countertop, there was a hole which held a briquette stove with two shelves which had to be rotated every four hours as the ambers cooled off. This was how the bedroom floor was heated and a boiling pot of water was always ready for us to use.

My first mishap with boiling water happened while I was rotating the stove shelf and the boiling pot was too heavy for me to lift; the hot water spilled over and tipped over onto my body. No one was there to help me so I stripped off my hot clothes and doused myself with ladled cold water which was by the door in a huge crock. No one knew that this had happened to me and I recovered over time. About a few months later, my grandmother had an adult party and we girls had to stay home. While we were playing with each other, Grandmother brought a relative to see our house. Suddenly Grandmother looked at all of us and said to me in a threatening way, "I'm going to send your mother away to be married and leaved you with no one." Soon, I was scared about Mom leaving us alone and I never told my mom about this.

Mom had finally found work as a seamstress in downtown Seoul. After she started working, she became a much happier person; up to this time she was depressed and withdrawn. With Mom working, I had to take on more responsibilities at home and I was unable to afford to go to school. While Mom was away from home, I was searching for a job for miles from home.

One summer night in the monsoon season, rain was pouring. As I was walking home, a policeman stopped me. He asked me where I was going. I explained to him where I lived and he stopped the bus and told the bus driver to take me to my destination. When I arrived home, Mom was waiting up for me. Her face was turning blue and she beat me badly. This was the first of many beatings I would receive from her but I did not have a clue as to why.

It was shortly after this night that we moved to a larger home owned by another wealthy family not related to us, higher up on the hill. My family lived in the rental quarters and it had its own kitchen and also had two kitchen doors, front and back. The outhouse was about 20 feet from the back door, and there was a large field where they planted vegetables to be sold as well to feed the family. They had a large family consisting of the matriarch, her two sons, her daughter, one daughter-in-law, and two grandsons.

My first impression of the matriarch was of a very stern and imposing wrinkled woman who took no gruff from anyone. She had complete rule over the entire household. Perhaps the reason she was inflexible with everyone was because she wanted to carry on in her husband's place and keep the family prestige alive. Her older son was married and had two sons. He was a gentle spirit who was a peacemaker along with his wife. They were kind, generous people, always showing their compassion toward others. On the other hand, the younger son and daughter were argumentative and only wanted do things their way. They were the opposite of their older brother. My family had been in this home less than a year, but they treated us like their own family; in fact, they treated us better than my grandmother and her extended family. Once we moved in with this family, I did not see my grandmother. For a while, I found myself having fun with this family, especially the daughter. Whether we realized or not, we found ourselves and became sisters by choice. We became inseparable and soon she found me a job where she worked. She was a fabric cutter for a clothing manufacturer. In the morning we left home together to go to work and in the evening we rode the bus together. On the bus, we talked about many other things in life, mostly small talk: what happened at work, who did what . . . most of the time we gossiped about someone at work and we giggled. At the same time, my mother and her younger brother became involved, but I did not know this right away. Finally, I had made a great friend and we were moving again, and it was 1970.

This time we moved further down the hill to a less rocky, more fertile part of the mountain. It was a peaceful, quiet, pretty, small community in the midpoint on the mountain. Most people in this community were middle-income families who shared everything with other members. I knew many people in this community because I delivered water to many of them to make money. I was up and down this mountain so many times and I knew every rock and all the trees. The house we lived in here was very tiny, and had one small window in the bedroom. Our bedroom from ceiling to floor was seven feet, and the square footage of the entire room was 10 feet by 10 feet, for all of us fit in one room (five girls and mother). In this home, the only entrance was opened onto the kitchen. The kitchen floor was dirt and when it rained, the roof leaked and made the floor into mud. In order to not walk in the mud, I had to stomp on the charcoal briquette (a briquette was the size of a gallon paint can, and it had 19 holes in it), to break it down to spread over the mud. Once it dried, I had to sweep the floor.

My mother still worked in the same place as a seamstress and she was gone most of the day. I, on other hand, became an entrepreneur at 12 years of age, selling crepe-like treats. I had to make ladles out of tin cans. In the ladles, I melted brown sugar and when it melted, put powdered soda so that it could rise. I would then turn it over onto a flat oiled metal sheet and then it flattened like a pancake. This sweet flavored treat I sold to schoolchildren after school in the playground. This was my job after Mom went to work. My mother was under the impression that I was attending school, but I actually stayed home to make the sweets in order to make money. My school didn't care whether I attended or not because my mother couldn't afford the tuition. Her monthly paycheck went to the rent, 100 pounds of flour, and a rice barley mix about 50 pounds, then some money set it aside for her to use for bus fare, make-up and her clothes. Once I had enough money from selling the sweets, I bought white rice, not mixed with barley, made for Mom because she wouldn't eat the other. I knew that Mom was always in pain in her stomach area before and after she ate anything, so this was my way of caring for her. Each night, I cooked rice and put it into a bowl which had a lid and wrapped it in the blanket so that it stayed warm until Mom returned home from work.

One day, coming home after work, I found a huge mess in the house. Apparently my sisters were hungry and tried to make lunch for themselves. They had opened the bag of flour and it was all over the kitchen and also in the bedroom. Not just that, their faces were covered with flour and they looked like ghosts. I knew when Mom saw this mess, she would be pretty upset. I started cleaning up. I was angry at my sisters, but they ran outside and hid in the alley. I managed to clean up all the mess my sisters made before nightfall. I made dinner for my sisters, cleaned them up, and put them to bed. *It was about 10:00 p.m. and soon Mom should be on the bus*, was my thought and I was anxious to get to the bus station. It was my ritual to go to the bus station to meet Mom and walk home with her. On the way home, uphill, we always held hands and talked about different things. She seemed to rely on me because I was oldest and she knew my sisters would be safe with me. I was only 12 years old and had too many responsibilities.

That winter, my mother suddenly received a visit from my cousin, Sung Chan's wife. As soon as she saw my mom, her eyes filled with tears. She was a very young woman who had a difficult marriage. She had a daughter, but she had to commit her to the Buddhist temple because Sung Chan had died and she could not care for her daughter. I overheard them talking about how my cousin had committed suicide because he did not want to go to jail for being AWOL from his service in Vietnam. She also told my mom about my father's brother who had been Chief of Police dying from alcoholism in his mistress' house. My other cousin was caught for stealing goods from homes and they cut off his hands and threw him in the jail. Our family saga seemed to be one tragedy after another. I listened further to their conversation and my cousin's widow wanted to stay in Seoul, so my mom was able to find a job for her as a live-in-maid. She worked for a while, but she couldn't handle her grief. She shaved her head and took vows to become a Buddhist monk. Having overheard all this brought back the memory I had repressed about what Sung Chan had done to me when I was nine years old.

After my cousin's widow left my young life was hardship shaped by Mom's influence, and its shades of darkness began to paint me with despair; I suffered much pain and agony from her malicious hands. The start of huge conflict between my mother and me was the night I went to meet her at the bus station. At the bus station, I looked in every bus that came every 10 minutes but she wasn't on any of them. Finally, the last midnight bus came and I decided to go home. As I was turning my head, I saw Mom get off the bus with a man, but she did not see me because it was dark and the stores were closed. They started walking the opposite direction from home so I decided to follow them. They crossed a footbridge. Under the bridge, there was a creek that ran through both sides of the bridge, with tall grass grown like marshland. I followed them a little further. There was the grayish-blue color of streetlights following them to a three-story building. It was a hotel. My heart was pounding and the chill came over me because the fear I hid deep in my heart began to surface and I saw her entering the building with him. I thought to myself, *Why is she going there?* I decided to go home. On the way, I felt betrayed by her. I did everything for her, cooking, cleaning, taking care of my sisters and making money trying to help her. I was angry but I couldn't show my anger to anyone, even myself.

I woke up in the middle of the night and I went to the outhouse. I got up from the bed and walked to the door. The moon shown through our bedroom's open window, and it illuminated my mother's sleeping area which had doubled in size. I realized she must have brought him home with her. I went into the kitchen and noticed a pair of man's shoes. I then clearly knew why she stopped at the hotel. When I woke up in the morning, he was already gone before we girls woke up. I never spoke with my mom about this incident and I felt that it was no use for me to wait for Mom every night at the bus station. I knew who this man was and I had a feeling that I could stop him from seeing Mom or coming home. I contacted his sister who I had become close with and I told her about her brother's meeting my mother. I told her because I was afraid of losing my mom. His sister must have told her family about what I said because the matriarch came to see my mother. I was at home when this woman showed up, and when she left my mother was in tears. My mother never said anything to me, but her attitude toward us changed dramatically. She started screaming at us for the littlest things. Soon, she started wearing more make-up, changing her appearance and not coming home on time, and she began to hit me as well as scream. Eventually, her turmoil, rage and her agony was put upon me and I became her scapegoat. Her frustration was my problem and I was her doormat whenever things did not go her way. She used her forceful rage all over my body with a half-size baseball bat. On top of all this, she lost her job and her beatings became more regular. My poor little body was always covered with colorful, ugly bruises. Wracked with pain from the beatings, I still had to deliver heavy water buckets during all kinds of weather. My small hands and feet were bleeding constantly because of blisters on my dry and cracked skin. The worst thing was that my hands and feet got frostbitten and swelled up like a balloon in the winter.

So often, she screamed at me, "You are miserable human garbage; I don't know why you were even born. Get out of my sight!" Then she struck me on the left side of my head with the bat which eventually caused hearing loss in my left ear. During all the beatings by my mother, I never showed tears or tried to escape her tirade. This was my way of showing her that I had strength, and I let her see how weak she was. I discovered that many years later from her sister that I used to go over to her house and sleep on the stairway after confrontations with my mom; other times, I got out of the room without breathing and cried in a narrow alley under the roof. When this happened the weather was usually rainy or cold in winter. I was a devoted, faithful, dutiful daughter but I wasn't enough for my mother, no matter whatever I tried to do to please her.

Since my mom lost her job because of me and I was somewhat

responsible, we had no money for food. Mom was too proud to ask her mother for help but also, my grandmother had given up her money for Mom's sister. I thought that Mom had given up trying to find the job, so I took it upon myself to look for food. The weather was turning bitter cold, so I would take a plastic bag and walk two or three miles to beg for food. I became a beggar. I woke up my sister Kyong Hie and walked with her door to door, and I talked with people that answered and asked them for food. A couple of generous people gave me a bag full of food, but I couldn't stop. I wanted to have a little more. So I knocked on other doors. At one house a lady appeared and asked us in. Her family was just having an early dinner and she asked us to join them. I'd said I couldn't because I was worried about my other sisters and my mom. She was insistent and we ended up eating there. When we were done, she gave us some money to buy charcoal and food, and she put more food into the bag. We thanked them and said good-bye.

When we got out of house, the sun was setting in the west. We hurried home and on the way there, I bought a few briquettes but the store owner was a kind man who gave me credit. I told him I would pay him back. I guess he knew our situation. When I got home, I started a fire and cooked dinner and also heated the house. Everyone was still sleeping under the blankets. I went to wake them up and feed them, but my mom couldn't eat because she was emotional about everything I had accomplished for family. That was the beginning of the end of the beatings, but also it was start of the separation of the entire family.

Between January and February of 1971, I was away from home. My mom found me a job as a door girl for a fancy sauna. A door girl opened the door for the rich people who came to the sauna. This building was located in downtown Seoul in the manufacturing district. It was a twelve-story building, and the sauna was located on the fifth and the sixth floors. I was placed on the sixth floor, which was the women's section and sometimes, I worked on the fifth floor for the men, if they were short on staff. My duties included giving out the tickets for the guests as they came in and the tickets for their shoe locker numbers. The numbers represented their status (such as actors and actresses, millionaires, businessmen, etc). I then took their shoes in the locker room, gave a few towels and a gown. After they changed their clothes, I waited for them outside the locker room to escort them through the whole floors, explaining all the different areas, and introducing them to the manager and the staff that would be working with them.

After turning them over to the staff, I went back to the main door to wait for the next guest to arrive. The sauna was open from 8 a.m. to 10 p.m., and was constantly busy. There were three shifts alternating hours for all girls working there. All the single staff members lived in the section of the sauna and we would have some time off every couple of months by rotation of our schedules. They paid me a salary and I also received large tips from the guests. I was actually too young to have this job; however, my mom's friend worked at the front desk of the fifth floor and she was able to get me hired. My mom always showed up on my payday and took my paycheck, plus, I gave her my tips. I kept nothing for myself, and if I needed clothes, she would buy them for me. I was given a uniform to wear at work, so I rarely needed anything. I do remember one outfit my mom bought for me. It was a pale yellow turtleneck shirt with a solid red pleated jumper and white tights. When she dropped this outfit off for me, I could not get over how old she looked. I examined her further: her hands were dry, cracked and wrinkled and her eyes were filled with moisture; she was trying to not to show her face to me.

In this place I made many friends but only one I felt close to. She was much older than me, a tall beautiful woman who liked me very much. We would go out to movies together and window shopping. We were also allowed to use some of the sauna facilities such as the racquetball court and gym. This was an ecstatic time in my life. I was working the morning shift and I saw an actress enter the door. Soon, I remembered the movie I saw a while ago, "The Home of the Stars." *A woman's miserable life, a life filled with scars and painted in darkness. She'd lived her life as best she could until the end. No one encouraged or gave her hope to live, but when she found herself, she could not live anymore. She had supportive parents, however; in fact, they were very understanding. They'd given her anything she wanted. She'd had it all, a roof over her head, food and an education through high school.*

While she was in high school, though, she met an attractive, brilliant, gentle young man. Her twinkling dark eyes were full of hope and happiness. Their love story was very special: powerful, sweet and passionate. No one could separate them. Then one day without warning, his wife came to see her. Suddenly the blue sky changed to a dark cloud over her head and she experienced the truth about him. She made a choice to break up with him and quit school. She left her lovely home forever. She walked around in a fog and had mixed feelings about love and her life experiences that eventually carried no direction in her life. She tossed herself in a place that she could ease the pain. The most valuable possession was her body as a woman, and she trashed herself, losing her virginity to someone she didn't love. With mixed emotions, she struggled but found a place to live and worked as a maid. The people gave her a live-in option of room and board, so she made little money. Slowly, time passed and she found the happiness she'd thought she had lost. She lived there several years. One rainy day, the owner of the house came into her room drunk and savagely raped her. She could not say anything to anyone. Feeling useless and alone, she had to run further away.

During blizzard weather, she met a handsome gentleman at a club. She was already drunk, and he didn't mind her behavior. He became interested in her. He listened carefully with an open heart. Soon they grew close to each other and shared an intimate relationship for a while. She found herself in love, but she could not love him because he was a well known writer in a high-class society, rich and charming. On the other hand, she was a prostitute. She had such low self-esteem that she decided to end their relationship. He was still sleeping soundly and she got up to write on the mirror, "I love you. Goodbye." Then she slipped away soundly forever.

She'd left him; she sank deeper and deeper to the bottom of the pit and could not get up anymore. She'd decided to let herself go from the world. It was a sunny, beautiful winter day. The snow was coming down steadily and piled up on the street. She wanted to see him once more and be with him one last time, but he did not know. They spent an incredible night together, and again, she left him while he was asleep. She walked toward the quiet river bend. Her feet sank in the deep, untouched, cotton white snow. As she walked, she grabbed a handful of snow and put it in her mouth and took sleeping pills with the melted snow. She got closer to the riverbank and imagined her first boyfriend once more and she saw he was running toward her waving wildly. She fell down and drowned in the river.

When the police found her in the river, they found a phone number in her pocket along with a letter to the writer. In the letter she'd written that she loved him very much but she couldn't receive his love and she wasn't worthy. She'd also instructed him that he could cremate her body and scatter her ashes into the river where she died. He did exactly what she wanted. When he scattered the ashes, he wept with a broken heart. How precious her life could have been if she could have understood how much he loved her!

I'd seen this film not long ago but when I saw the actress in my workplace, I was stunned. Ironically, my life seemed like this movie and had a strong impact on me; yet, I did not know what kind of life waited for me in years to come. I had vacation time coming and I went home. It was around January of 1973, and I was in for the shock of my young life. I took the bus home, and when I arrived, I went to see my grandmother. My grandmother was surprised to see me, but she didn't show any emotion. Soon, my mom arrived to see me. I asked her where my sisters were and she said she had sent them to live with other family members because she couldn't provide for them anymore. When I heard what she said, I was very sad and angry because I gave her enough money to support my family. However, I never brought this matter up to her. Since I had nowhere to stay, I took the bus back to the sauna. It was very late night when I arrived. The next morning, we were at the breakfast table. My good friend told me that during the night I was calling for my dad, sitting up in the corner of the room; I'd cried, then went back to sleep.

Shortly after this incident, I was forced to leave my job because of a law had passed that anyone under 18 years old could not work in public places so my mom found me a job again. The lady who originally got me the job at the sauna recommended me as a maid to her neighbor. Since my mom knew the lady's mother, she was aware of my new position and showed up every payday again and took my paycheck. Now that I think about it, she was like a human bloodsucker, but I never hated her or disobeyed her because, after all, she was still my mother. The second job I found was as a live-in maid. The family was small but they had a large house. In this house, I was constantly beaten by the woman of this house. No matter how well I tried to please her, she wasn't satisfied. The wife was a tyrant and exercised great power over me when her husband wasn't home. I can't tell how many times she scolded me without reason because I was a weak child. Each time this happened, I embraced myself and wept in the kitchen.

Since I was forced to use very cold water to wash clothes by hand and wash dishes outside of the kitchen, I developed frostbitten hands and feet, which swelled up and cracked open. One morning in winter, I carried the breakfast table to the room and her husband saw the condition of my hands and feet. He told his wife to get some garlic and soak them in hot water. When it got soft, she put my hands and feet in the garlic water. He said to do it often, especially at night before I went to bed. He also said that my hands and feet would heal in no time. I told the lady who got me the job about the abuse I was receiving from her neighbor. I figured that she must have mentioned it to my mom. Next thing I knew, my mom called on the phone and told me I would be leaving this job and that she had found me another job.

In the fall of 1973, I went to work at the restaurant, Seragon. The restaurant was run by my grandmother's friend. He knew all my family pretty well and I was treated better by him. However, my hours were very long and I only got about three hours sleep a day, seven days a week. The pay wasn't good, but I received large tips. My mother was still taking it, but the restaurant fed me well. I stayed at the restaurant about a year, then found a better paying job at a coffee shop in 1974. However, in the coffee shop, I had to sleep on the cement floor using the cushions from the chairs along with the other workers at night after closing up. I was about 15 years old and had blossomed into a shapely young lady. This job allowed me to dress like a businesswoman. I began getting attention from the male customers. The hours were long, but time went by faster because I didn't get bored with this job. I enjoyed the attention I was receiving because it was the first time in my life that I received complements about my work and looks. A lot of men wanted to have me sleep with them, but I couldn't give myself away.

Even though I was happy, I felt something was missing. I yearned for a home of my own and my family altogether, someone to care for me. Suddenly I became overwhelmed emotionally and decided to take some sleeping pills. I had purchased some over the counter and I took a half bottle and went to sleep. Next morning, when the others woke up to the start the day they noticed I wasn't getting up.

Three

I really don't remember anything else after taking the pills. Someone must have called my mother because the next thing I remembered I was on the bus with my mom who had found me another job as a maid. While we were on the bus, she snapped at me saying, "Why didn't you kill yourself, it would be really nice for me and you?" I was just human garbage roaming around in the dirt and taking up space in a hostile world. I did not know why I was even born, and why I had to go on living. I was just walking aimlessly in the darkness. I was screaming for help, but no one heard my scream,; I was searching, but no one knew what I was searching for, even myself.

The home my mom found me a job in was memorable even now. The woman's name was Mrs. Park, who lived with her husband and her college-aged daughter, Won Ae, and a son who was away in the Navy, an officer. Mrs. Park had other children from a previous marriage but she took care of them like her own. Although they were grown and had married, they also had their own children. Some lived nearby in Korea and others lived in California and New York. The Parks were millionaires. Their house was gigantic and they had three maids and a chauffeur. They were extremely rich, but they were also the most generous people I had ever met. She had a gracious smile on her face and she never raised her voice no matter what. She wanted her workers to be happy and always deeply cared for everyone under her roof. Mrs. Park and her husband loved me very much, and did not hit me or scold without reason. I was their adopted daughter because I was treated exactly like their own daughter. I was very happy there even though it was long hours of work, but it was my choice. I called her "Mom" and before she went to bed, I used to give her a massage until her husband arrived. Sometimes, I gave Mr. Park a massage and he gave me extra money. In her home, there was much I could learn from them about family ties. They were all happy people and grateful with every moment in their lives. They were socially respected, harmonized with each other's roles publicly and privately. Mr. Park was a sophisticated and wise man with a successful business. He was well-mannered with every class of person. Mrs. Park was a confident woman who tried to maintain the integrity of her pleasant surroundings. Their daughter, Won Ae, was a sweet, unassuming intelligent girl who was compassionate. When she was in her first year of college, I used to wait for her outside of the college gates. This made me so happy and I adored her like the older sister I never had. When she got out of class, we walked home together and chatted and giggled all the way, just the way I used to walk home with my mom.

Won Ae had everything. She had a loving, caring family, her own beauty, intelligence and a devotion to higher education. It was a nonstop learning process for me. Every night she would teach me English, how to read and write. I memorized all the consonants and vowels. I learned everything from her, which got me interested in learning different languages. Not only did she have everything, but she served God, absolutely beyond criticism from her parents. Her parents were disapproving of her religious beliefs, yet, many years later her mom became a Christian who served God dearly. Then there was Won Ae's brother, who was serving his country as a Naval Officer. This family was a perfect, unbroken circle. I admired these people and thought of them as a model of a great family who supported each other in everything. I had no problem with the family. Mrs. Park gave me a paycheck for less than $10 a month, but it was a lot of money in the 1970's. I felt comfortable with everyone and I began to ease years of my pain in my body. Often, while I was cleaning I fell asleep on the stairs, because my mind was relaxed and emotionally, I wasn't uptight any more.

My mom still came every moth and took my earnings. I didn't need to go anywhere and if I needed to go to somewhere, the chauffeur came to pick me up. I was the youngest maid and cared for very much. While I was there, I was never hungry and I was given choices of things to eat. Sometimes, Mrs. Park took me to places I could enjoy. I saw an ice skating show when American ice dancers toured Korea and that was my first real American play on ice. Mrs. Park often traveled to the United States to visit her mother and brother in California, and also her home was nonstop filled with visitors from everywhere.

Time had passed quickly. In my heart, I craved for love and wanted to be with my family. I was an unloved young girl whose heart was steeped in sadness, and when the night fell, I lay under the blanket feeling very lonely. Deep in the night, my tears were saturated on my pillow just about every night, and some nights I looked at all those houses with lights on and wished to have a home with my mom, dad and four lost sisters and tears would start falling down like the summer rain. I began to realize there was no hope for me to go home, so I struggled to forget about my mom and sisters but there were more things to deal with and that was my emotional rage. I thought I was living the good life, but I wasn't. I was pretending that everything was alright.

I could not stay at Mrs. Park's house any longer. I was with a great family for several years but I made the choice to leave because I was becoming depressed. What I experienced with Parks made a conflict inside of me. Maybe it was envy of what they had, and I wished I could have it, too. I left with the clothes on my back and without speaking to anyone because I couldn't express feelings inside of me. That particular afternoon, I shopped around in a few stores for sleeping pills again and walked around somewhere in a flea market, not very far away from Mrs. Park.

I bought a can of 7-Up and took the pills. I was walking around in a daze. I just wanted to die. I just wanted to lay my head down somewhere and never wake up. I remember being in a dark, narrow alley and someone grabbing me and leading me into a small confined room where he made me lay down on the floor. I could smell the liquor on his breath. He started to touch me. I got up and ran away. I was still groggy from the pills, but I could feel the mist on my face from the early morning weather. I had some money, so I bought a daily newspaper. I found an employment agency and went there. The agency set up some appointments for me with people who needed a maid. This agency charged me a placement fee, which meant my first check would go to them. Someone came over to the agency and took me to their home but I ran away after a few hours because her house was different from Mrs. Park's. I searched for work as a maid in a few more places but nothing felt right, so I decided to call Mrs. Park on my own. She told me to come over and when I arrived, her daughter Won Ae was waiting for me and hit me with a rolled up magazine. She was very upset with me for leaving without a word. Then Mrs. Park came and said to me, "I treated you like a daughter, but you betrayed me." I didn't respond— I just knelt in front of her with my head down in tears.

Finally, she must have felt sorry for me and she gave me another chance. She said that her stepdaughter was looking for someone. Her stepdaughter had just had a baby and she needed help. Mrs. Park asked if I was interested. I took the job because I felt obligated and had nowhere else to go. From the minute I started working there, the stepdaughter, Kum Ja, and her husband were constantly arguing. Her husband was trying to please his wife, but nothing he did was good enough for her. I believe she only put up with me because Mrs. Park was a constant visitor. I worked there about six months, until my mother showed up. Again, she took my paycheck every month.

After about a year of working at Kum Ja's, I overslept one day in winter. The water pipes were frozen, their house had no heat, and I couldn't make their breakfast. Her husband went to work without having a meal or being able to wash anything. Many things were beyond my control that day. After her husband went to work, Kum Ja was extremely upset with me. She could not control her anger. She backhanded me and clawed my face with her long skinny nails under my chin and drew blood. I could not deal with her hysteria, so I tried not to antagonize her the rest of the day. I was beaten all the time by strangers instead of my mother. These were unforgivable actions done by evil human beings on my body. Later that day, Kum Ja called me to come to see my mom who showed up to collect my pay. The only time I saw my mom, in any month, was when my paycheck was in the palm of her hand. My mom saw my face was peeled off, and yet, she did not give me any protection with any comforting words. She said nothing, just took my check and left. Finally, Kum Ja's husband came home and things were normal again.

A few days later, I was washing diapers in the bathroom tub. The water was running in the tub, and I was bent over the washboard. In front of me, there was a ceramic sink. I must not have heard Kum Ja call me. The next thing I knew, she came up behind me and kicked me in the middle of my back, causing my head to slam into the ceramic sink. I was gasping for breath as I tried to stand. I thought my back was broken and I was in great pain. She started yelling about something as she walked away to fetch the baby. I finished rinsing the diapers and hung them up to dry. My heart was filled with tears, but my eyes were dry as a bone. My rage, which had been building up for years, finally reached the surface.

It had snowed quite a bit that day so I went out in the afternoon to shovel the snow. While I was shoveling, I had a lot of time to think about my situation. I thought to myself that I would never let anyone hurt me again or take my money again. I made the decision

39

to leave that afternoon. I dropped the shovel and left with only the clothes on my back again.

I ran to a little mom and pop store nearby that I used to go to, and asked them if they could find me a job. The store owner knew me well and I explained to her what had happened. The store owner told me about a customer whose daughter was getting married soon, and that they would need some help. Plus, they planned to relocate after their daughter's wedding. The store owner called the customer and recommended me. Soon, they arrived at the store and agreed to take me with them. I explained my situation with Kum Ja to them and they agreed that I could stay in the home until after the wedding and the move. They seemed to be nice people, but work was hard. I felt much happier and I was able to forget about Kum Ja, Mrs. Park and my mother.

The wedding and the move were finally complete and we settled in the new home in a very wealthy neighborhood. I lived in the house while the newlyweds were on their honeymoon. While they were away, I had been sleeping in their bedroom. I heard they were coming home and I had to move to another bedroom. It was across from the master bedroom. Their five year old son was sleeping soundly when I entered the room. When the newlyweds returned, their parents threw them a huge welcoming party. The mother of the bride drank too much as usual, and she was staggering all over the place in their home. She made a scene of herself and then left on her own accord. I waited for her to return home, but she did not. When all guests had left, it was after midnight. There was a phone call, and her husband picked up the phone. I assumed his wife was on the phone and I saw her husband get very upset. I had to clean up without anyone's help. The father of the bride asked me how I felt, and I slightly nodded my head and said, "I'm fine." It was very early in the morning when I retired. I was exhausted from being on my feet all day.

Falling asleep, I heard the door open, and the father came into the room. He asked me if I needed anything. I told him my back was hurting and I was aching everywhere in my body. He said, "I have something for you to rub on your back." Then, he went quickly out of the room and brought a few pain pills and cream for me. He asked me where the pain on my back was and he put cream on it. He massaged my back for a few minutes and soon, I fell asleep. I woke up with an uneasy feeling. Again, it was the second time in my life I had experienced a man's hands on my body and his other hand closed over my mouth. This time, I shook off his hand and ran out and threw myself into his daughter and son-in law's room, while they were soundly sleeping. They woke up in shock, and asked me what had happened. Both of them were looking at the wall clock, and said, "It is 4 o'clock." I told them what had happened and they let me stay with them the rest of the night. They remained calm until their mom returned home early in the morning.

When the mother returned, her daughter told her what had happened a few hours earlier, and without question, my beatings started again. She dragged me from one room to another room and the room door sills were 3ft. high. I smelled her breath, which was disgusting, and her face was still red from the alcohol. She threw me into the master room, where her husband kept himself perfectly composed. Because of her savage beatings, my face was swollen and red, my hair was a mess, and as if that wasn't enough, she grabbed my little shoulder and shook my whole body, calling me a whore. My upper body was bruised everywhere, especially under the armpit. I was wearing a purple, thick winter sweater and the friction of the thread made my skin peel off and it caused bleeding on my underarms.

The savage beatings were done. She told me to get out of the house. I packed my things and took the bus back to the store owner. I explained to them what had happened. They fed me and calmed me down. Within a few minutes, the father of bride showed up and

41

handed me an envelope. He must have been following me from the moment I left his home. I opened the envelop. It must have been a month's wages and it was generous. He told me he was sorry, and the store owner raised hell with him. When he left, I thanked the store owners and said goodbye to them. Since I had money, I just wanted to rest my body for a few days. I rented a motel room for a few days and I was planning on looking for another job.

I rested a day or two and then woke up with hunger. I thought I might grab a bite and look for a job, but instead, I searched the drugstore. It was a crisp, arctic cold day. My hand stuck to every drugstore doorknob that I opened. My whole body was still aching from the beating, and my sweater was still stuck to the underarms from the drying blood. I did not have a warm jacket or boots, and still I hadn't eaten in I didn't know how many days. I felt a chill all over my body and by evening, I had purchased enough sleeping pills. Once more, I entered the store and bought a can of 7-Up, and I gulped down a handful of the pills. I didn't feel hungry anymore. Matter of fact, I forgot about how cold my body was. In that an arctic cold I walked a little more without knowing where I was going.

I was just 17 years old and still trying to take my life for myself. The next thing I remember is that I fell on the road at an intersection. I thought I had to stand up and wanted to cross the road, but I could not get up. I could feel nothing from my waist down. I thought, if I could just cross the intersection, I could make it to the police station on the other side of the road but I must have blacked out. When I woke up, I was in a room with four white walls and I was lying on a metal bunk bed and no one was there with me. A few minutes later, a woman police officer entered the room. I asked her where I was, and she said I was at the Police Station. The officer told me I had been there for two days. The officer said that I had no identification and she had already made arrangements with someone to take me somewhere. The officer unlocked the straps which were on my arms and feet. Then the officer questioned me about what had happened and why. I told the officer where I had been working, and everything that I had gone through to take my life. A few hours later, the husband of the woman who had beaten me showed up at the Police Station. The officer took him to the other room and they talked, but I did not have a clue what they talked about, then he was gone. I did not know what justice was but it was injustice done to me without any compensation. I could ask no one for help, not even the law. I thought the law was supposed to protect innocent victims, but he got away. I was a girl who roamed around the earth taking up space for no reason, with no purpose.

After the man left from the Police Station, the officer took me to a house somewhere through several different alleys. There, a man and woman waited for me. I did not ask where I was going nor did the officer explain who these people were. I was terrified, but I had no choice. They asked me to sit on the floor and gave me a blanket to cover my cold body. They fed me a warm, delicious meal. Now that I think about it, they must have been youth social workers in Korea. I think the organization was called B.B.S. (I would like to find out someday who they were). Both the man and woman asked me many questions such as if I had parents and where I lived. I told them that my parents were dead and I didn't have a home. I told them I was dropped from the sky and was on my own and no one knew me. The social worker then asked me if there was anyone I knew of that they could contact. I thought of Mrs. Park and gave them her phone number. When they hung up with her, they told me that they felt Mrs. Park was a nice person and she also told them to take good care of me. I thought that would be the last time I had heard about Mrs. Park, but many years later I would meet her again.

The social workers asked me what I desired most at this time and I told them that my only desire was to sleep forever. One of them arranged for a room for me at a motel and I slept there for two days without waking up. On the third day, one of them visited me and told me that he arranged for someone to take care of me now and that this person would find me a job, too. He left me a phone number and I was waiting in a motel.

By afternoon, another person came to take over the case. He was very nice to me and took me to a place where I could find a job, but I didn't like it. The place had the look of a jail and I felt scared. All the young men were wearing some kind of uniform and they were cutting wood with a huge machine and it made a loud noise. He took me to a few different places to find work but I did not like any of them. Toward the evening, he fed me and took me to a movie. He wanted to take my mind off killing myself again. So I went with him wherever he took me. After the movie, it was very late and we had to find a place to sleep.

We took the bus and crossed the Han River. In the bus I saw the light glittering in the water and I was able to breathe. We got out of the bus and we walked through a large flea market. On the corner of the market, there was a motel light on. He rented a motel room and he showed me where he would be sleeping. I discovered this social worker was wearing a double showing mask on one side during the day, and at night, he turned into a human beast. He wore thick magnifying glasses. His face was pockmarked, and he had an evil look on under the night light. I felt very intimidated by this man, and he gave me the creeps. I fell asleep, but I do not remember how long I had been sleeping when I felt something crawling up my arm. I woke up with a start and noticed that the social worker was sitting above my head and touching my arms. I jumped out of the bed and ran down the stairs to the front office of the motel. I pounded on the door and woke up the motel owner. She was a single woman soundly sleeping and woke up with a shock. In the dark, she asked, "Who is it?" and I said, "Open the door." She turned on the light and opened the door. She settled me down and questioned me. I explained the situation with the social worker and what he tried to do. Right away, she went to the room and told him to leave and never return. I was in the front office and saw him leave. Then the motel owner fed me and let me sleep in the office with her.

The next morning, she woke me up, and she asked many questions about my situation. She then offered me a job at the motel until she could find something suitable for me. She said she could not pay me, but would give me room and board. Every meal she made for me was sumptuous and delicious, and the meal was always warm. I stayed with that motel owner for a month. I was still underage by law, so she asked around the neighborhood if someone needed a maid. Across from the motel, there was an independent owner who operated a dressmaking shop. In the shop, they had at least four or five employees. They measured bodies, designed, cut fabrics and sewed. After getting more familiar with the businesses in the area, I asked the motel owner if she would ask the dressmaker about getting a job for me. It seemed like a decent place for me to work and I did have some experience with sewing, but there was not much I could brag about. I told the motel owner that I was a very quick and willing learner. So, she talked to the dressmaker. Soon, the motel owner took me to meet the dressmaker. The dressmaker liked me right away, but she wanted me to work in her home instead of working in the shop. I thanked the motel owner and told her that I would never forget her hospitality and said my goodbyes.

In the late afternoon, the dressmaker took me to her home. She lived in a penthouse apartment. She reminded me of Mrs. Park and I felt comfortable being there right away. I felt like I knew her from some time ago, somewhere. I met her mother and her five year old son. She explained to me that her husband was an officer in the Korean Army. She said that he was away most of the year and sometimes she would visit him. She also said that he would be coming home within a few months. I realized that it was almost the end of the year. I was happy with this family. I seemed to please them because there were no beatings, and the family members were only three, therefore I did not have much work to do. My body needed a rest, even for a few hours a day.

In this home, my top priority was to make lunch and deliver it to the shop everyday. Everyone at the shop enjoyed my cooking and I was always praised for it. Sometimes after lunch, I stayed in the shop for practicing the sewing and cutting fabrics. I had a little fun, but I discovered that I did not want to do this job forever because I remembered that my mother was a seamstress. Sometimes, the dressmaker asked me to wait for her because she wanted me to be her company during the bus rides. I waited for her until the shop was closed. The shop closed usually about 10:00 p.m. and we would take the bus home. While we were on the bus, she asked personal questions about my life. She thought that it was unusual for a young woman like me, and sometimes, I had tears in my eyes. Then, I turned my head quickly the other way so that she could not see my tears. We had to cross a bridge over the Han River, and I remember how the city lights glittered beautifully on the water.

New Year's arrived soundlessly, and my happiness was short-lived as her husband returned home. Her husband bought a home where he was stationed so the family could be together. The dressmaker offered me to come live with them, but I wanted to stay in Seoul, even though I hated it. I had to stay in Seoul and find another job. If I did not find a job, I would be homeless. In the city was where I belonged, and there was always plenty of work for me, but also I wished that I could have had a day off so that my body could rest.

Four

When I reached 16 years old, it was a major turning point of my life; something was about to happen, but I did not know what. I desperately needed some money and a place to stay. I did not want to work as a maid or in a coffee shop anymore. After the considerable amount of thought, I picked up a newspaper and skimmed through the ads. An ad caught my eye and it said: "Make a lot of money, meet influential people, no manual work, get up late, etc." After a few minutes of thought, I dialed the agency. It was located in an exclusive area of Myung Dong, Seoul. The agent who answered the phone and told me that the ad I mentioned was all true. Then he gave me instructions on how to get there. He told me to put on makeup and dress nicely and meet him in the coffee shop near the agency. I finally arrived as an excited naïve teenager. He ordered a cup of coffee for me and he was full of compliments about my looks. He asked if I had any experience with men. I had no idea what that meant, but I told him I had experience with men. I lied because I needed a place to stay. I had no idea what I was getting into.

He asked me to wait at the table and went to make a phone call. He came back and we talked for awhile. He asked me about my parents and my answer was I was alone, an orphan. He said that someone was coming to take me to a place to work. While we were talking, the coffee shop door opened and a stocky woman entered. He waved at her and excused himself for a few minutes. He sat with her at another table while they talked. He waved at me. He came back with her and introduced me. As he left, he said, "Good luck." The woman told me to come with her. We took a taxi and rode for about half an hour. The taxi stopped on the main street and she paid the taxi fare. We walked the street for a few minutes. I saw a huge sign on the wall: U.S.O. Army. I did not know it was the city of Young-San, Seoul. Her home was small, but it had two stories. As soon as I stepped into the bedroom, I noticed many girls sitting around, either watching TV or putting on their makeup. The phone rang, and a girl answered it. She asked who was available and said into the phone that she would send someone directly. I was asked to take a shower and do my hair and makeup. When I was all done, another girl gave me a nice suit to wear. At this point, I still had no idea what my job would be. The stocky woman told me to have dinner with her and I ate. Then she told me to just wait because my chance would come. While I was waiting, I realized that every time the phone rang, a girl would leave the place.

It was my turn. The owner told me I would be going with another girl. I did not ask questions and I just followed another girl. The girl and I got on the bus and finally arrived at a hotel in the City of Westgate in Seoul. I still had no clue what I was there for. We passed the hallway and went to the lobby at the front desk. At the front desk, a girl gave us two keys, and said that he was waiting for us. The girl who took me to the hotel asked me to follow her. She led me into a hallway, and I thought to myself, *This is a very long and dark hallway*. She gave me a key and told me go into the room. She would be down the hall in another room.

When I opened the door, the man was sitting on the couch. The night light was dimmed. On the table, many empty beer bottles were lined up neatly. He said to me, "Please come sit next to me." I was a little nervous but I went closer and sat next to him. He was about 40 years old; his face was ruddy and drunk. He told me to take a shower, and when I got out of the shower, he was laying on the bed naked. He told me to lay next to him. He proceeded to get on top of me and tried to kiss me. I turned my face immediately, but he held my shoulder down and entered me. I could not breathe. I was in excruciating pain and I screamed. As my screams got louder, he thought I was enjoying his savage sex. I was still a virgin and lost what was priceless. I was in so much pain, but managed to push him away. He fell off the bed and he did not get up.

Hurriedly, I grabbed my clothes in the dark, and I ran to the desk. The desk clerk called the room and the man must have said to let me go. The desk clerk handed me $5.00. The night was long and the daylight would arrive in a few more hours. I had nowhere to go because of the Korean curfew, so I decided to wait outside on the hotel steps until daylight arrived. During my long wait, I decided to run. I took the first bus that came and headed for In-Chun, where the ocean was. It was April 5th, 1975; I will never forget the date.

While on the bus, I had time to think. I thought about everyone I had encountered, and I started hating them and myself. I saw no light at the end of the tunnel. I felt like I was living in hell. I thought about how I never had my childhood. I should have been enjoying being young, but before I could bloom, I was engulfed by many evil humans. Furthermore, my experience with that drunken man made me scared of men in general. I cursed that drunken man for my entire trip to In-Chun. The bus dropped me off at Seoul Train Station. At the station, I had enough money to purchase a ticket to In-Chun. This place was near the ocean and I felt that I should be near the water. This was the trip that made the change in my life complete and set the stage for an entirely different adulthood.

As I watched scenery from the train window, I saw the mesmerizing views that I had only heard of. On the other hand, I saw the ugliness of the city that visitors would never see. As the train left the city behind, I saw the rivers, sandy beaches, rice patties and remote villages. It was such a beautiful place, but I never knew it existed. The further I traveled from Seoul, the more I felt the need to keep going wherever my destination might be. It seemed to me I was traveling away from my past and any guilt I felt. At last, with all the anticipation I felt, I hurriedly got off the train. The air was warm, damp and filled with smells of saltwater and fish. It was only April, but it felt like a summer day. The sun was rising and the air was thick with heavy fog while I was standing on the train platform. Standing there, I felt invited by the atmosphere of this part of Korea. I followed the other people who were disembarking into the station.

As I surveyed my surroundings, I could see a tall and large casino that stood upon the hill. Across from the station, there were many big and small clubs, coffee shops, restaurants, and many little shops along the street bottom of the hill. I was standing at the curb; there were many buses, taxis and people with bicycle-drawn carts who were selling breakfast. The rich butter smell from the cart made my stomach growl, so I purchased a breakfast sandwich from one of the carts. While enjoying my breakfast, I spoke with the owner and asked where I could go to see the ocean. The owner explained in full detail about the area where I was heading. He also told me which number bus to take and where it would drop me off. The people seemed much friendlier here than the big city where I left behind, I thought.

I hopped on the bus and told the bus driver where my stop should be. The bus driver applied politely that I should be sitting closer to him in order for me to get out of the bus. The bus would be packed with people as he traveled further south. The bus driver was right. Getting off the bus was a nightmare but anyhow, I arrived at the Yun On Boardwalk. This place was surrounded by seawater. The soft wind blowing from the sea moistened my face. I smelled the musky scent of the ocean and the spring tide was out. The surface of the sea floor was jet black, but also it invited those who were clam diggers. The clam diggers were carrying a wicker basket on their back and they squatted down. Their hands were occupied with the sea floor. All along the boardwalk, the vendors were opening their markets where they sold fresh ocean catch. Then, every 15 minutes, a new bus load of people arrived. Fishing ships were also arriving with more fresh supplies to the vendors, and they were happy to brag about how they did while on the sea.

I started walking down the boardwalk and I was in awe of everything that was happening around me. I had no time to be sad or worry about what would happen to me next. I just felt the moment, the moment where everything had stopped and I could be there forever. I felt that something was lifted from my chest like there was ventilation in my lungs. I felt so good being there that I could have stayed there all day. I enjoyed my freedom for the first time in my life. It was about lunchtime and I stopped at the indoor fish market and walked around. I found the restaurant that served fresh fish. I ordered a plate of raw fish, but when the fish arrived on my table, I was surprised by the portion of the fish. In the city, I could not order a plate of raw fish with the amount of money I paid at the restaurant. It was an incredibly fabulous lunch.

As I was enjoying my lunch, I also observed the people around me. People were surrounded by the tables and the first thing struck me was how loud these people were. They spoke different dialects, and on the table, there were many bottles of hard alcohol. These people seemed to be uneducated fishermen, but they were living simple lives not as complicated as my own. They had darker skin, wind-toughened faces from the weather and their hard lives. These men, who arrived from the ships, started drinking early in the afternoon. The more they drank, the louder they got and I enjoyed watching their antics. Eventually, they noticed me because I stuck out like a sore thumb. At one of the tables a man offered me a drink. I waved at him and told him, thank you but I could not drink. These people all looked at me because I was pale complexioned compared to them and I spoke Seoul Korean.

After lunch I decided to take a bus to one of the other areas nearby, and again, enjoyed the ocean air and observing the surroundings and the people. It was getting late and soon night was falling when I arrived at the town where the train station was. I noticed many neon lighted buildings on a hill near the station. I decided to go to one of the clubs to ask if they needed a hostess. This club needed hostesses to sit with male customers to keep them spending money. The club owner looked at me and offered me a job on the spot. The owner said that they kept any money spent in their club, and if the customer asked to take me out, I could keep anything he gave me.

The owner showed me where I would be staying and mentioned meals were included as long as I was there. The club had an upstairs and downstairs filled with tables. The owner introduced me to the other girls and gave me a Korean folk dress to wear for that evening only, and we planned on going shopping the next day. There were many working girls waiting in one of the upstairs rooms. These girls were smoking, playing cards, and the familiar scenery I saw a day before I left behind. As customers requested company, they would come and take their pick. Since I was the new girl in the club, I was selected right away, and I noticed everyone who came into this club was wearing black uniforms with a bow tie. These men were from the casino across the street and they were casino dealers. After spending the first night with one of these dealers in the club, all the dealers had to come to check this new girl out for their curiosity. I was kept very busy and the owner loved me dearly. The first night I received pretty good tips and I did not have to share it with anyone. Money was all for myself. I started making money for the club; the owner took me shopping for clothes at the best shop in the sailors' town. The club owner favored me from the beginning, and I believe because of this adoration, the other girls were envious of me. Therefore, I never became friends with any of them. No matter what went on around me, I was immensely happy there.

As I got comfortable with a new environment, I would disappear frequently without telling anyone. I got up very early, before the sun rose. I took the bus to the boardwalk. I felt that this was the only place I could share what was in my heart. In this place, I found a flat rock and I would sit peacefully and watched the seagulls soaring over my head. It seemed to me they knew I needed company. My eyes were busy looking at the harbor, at all the ships of different styles and sizes were coming and going. At times, I gazed on the people who were cracking oysters on the rocks. I enjoyed being out there because I could lose myself to my imagination; I closed my eyes to hear the heartbeat, and on the short, the sound of the waves lapping the beach, and slapping over the rocks. I had been coming here several months already, and if I could I would visit this place as many days as possible.

On one evening, I had too much to drink and I decided to get some fresh air. I got out and sat on the steps of the hotel next door to the club. All of a sudden, I felt something land behind me. In curiosity, I looked up and there was a man who I seemed to recognize as a customer. His name was Kim Gie. I did see him a couple of times, but I was not fond of him. Surprisingly, he asked me if I wanted to come up to his room, and on second thought, I thought, *Sure, why not?* I talked to the club owner and made a tray of drinks and food. He knew what to expect to have me on his arm for the night. I agreed and went to his room. When he answered the door, I thought to myself, *This is the most handsome man I have ever seen.* He smiled at me, took the tray of drinks and asked me in. We started talking and shared the drinks. I sat on his lap. I saw him a few times before but I had never felt such closeness until that night. Even though I was drunk he helped me to forget about the evil night in Seoul where I lost my virginity. Kim Gie was compassionate and tender in a way I had never experienced before.

In his tenderness, I briefly remembered my dad. He was a popular, well established dealer at the casino with many friends. He was tall and thin, with big brown eyes and straight thick black hair like my dad. We enjoyed each other's company absolutely every moment we were together. He made arrangements for me to bring drinks to his room almost every night after he got off from work. I would usually end up spending the night with him and pretty much I was his girl.

I do not know what possessed me, but I decided to contact Mrs. Park after being away for two years. The next thing I knew, my mother showed up at the door. She arrived one morning and spoke with the club owner. The owner said to me that someone was waiting outside for me. The club owner did not tell me it was my mother. I thought, *Maybe it's Mr. Kim and he may taking me somewhere.* My heart was full of excitement and I opened the door. I was stunned by the sight of my mother. She looked young, her hair was shoulder length and she was well dressed in a black business suit. She started crying when she saw me. I took her to a nearby coffee shop where we could talk. She seemed shocked that I was working at a club and assumed I was no longer a virgin. This seemed to be important to her. We had coffee, and then I took her to the nearby McArthur Park in In-Chun. It was the first time our pictures were taken by a photographer in front of McArthur's statue. Her visit was brief and by evening, she had taken a train back home. During Mom's visit, I blocked out all the old feelings of hatred I had for her. After her unexpected visit, I decided to run again because I did not want to repeat the old pattern with my mom. I told the club owner I was leaving and she wished me well and told me I could come back anytime. I left without telling Kim Gie that I was leaving.

The next club was in the city where the naval officers frequently visit and was about 30 minutes away from where I'd just left. This club was not as classy as the one I had just left; however, it paid me more and the place was run by a small family. This family had a strict separation between business and family. The club owners were husband and wife and had two children. They had an eight year old boy and ten year old girl. Besides owning the club, the husband had another job. In the club, three girls worked, including me. The owner treated us kindly and we were respected as family members. The owner trusted us to run the club for the family, and the owner rarely showed up during business hours. Every morning, I would give them the earnings from the previous night. Then, they left us money to restock the bar and kitchen. When the club closed at midnight, we were free to do whatever we desired.

In the winter of 1977, I was in the kitchen behind the counter, talking and preparing the next order for the customer who was sitting at the table. The door to the club opened, and a man who seemed familiar to me entered. He stared at me for sometime and then came to the counter and said to me that I looked familiar to him. After I heard his voice I realized he was the social worker who with his wife had taken care of me in Seoul briefly, after I had attempted suicide the second time. I served him a drink and asked him if he would wait for me until closing so we could reminisce. His response was that he could not stay, but he left me a phone number where he was staying and told me to call him. After closing the club I called him. He told me to come to his room so we could talk. I was drunk when I arrived. I do not remember how it happened exactly, but I remember me wanting to be with this man that night. Even though he was shy, he was happy being with me that night. Somehow, I sensed that this would be the only time we would be together, so I told him not to feel guilty. The next day we had breakfast together before he returned to Seoul.

It was about three weeks after he had returned to Seoul and I discovered I was pregnant. I knew he was the father because he was only man I had been with. Working at the club did not mean I had to sleep with every man who came into the club, and besides, I received a salary for just being there. At first, I was elated that I could be a mother; however, I started remembering my unhappy life as a child. A few days of engrossed thought made me wonder how could I bring life into my world, and how could I take care of a child. It was my responsibility for a child's life and I firmly told myself that I could not have this baby. No matter how hard it was to make the decision, I had to be unsentimental about an abortion. In Korea, an OB/GYN doctor could perform abortions in their office, and I found a doctor's office near where I worked. I talked to the doctor and he examined me and verified I was pregnant. We discussed my situation and he agreed to perform the abortion. The first baby lived less than a month in my womb and had to leave. After the procedure, the club owners gave me a room in their home to recover. I did not work for a few days. When I did return to work, I had restrictions about not drinking or lifting heavy things. I did not exactly follow the doctor's orders, however; I ended up paying the price for it, and yet, I kept working. The owners and other two girls kept telling me to take it easy, but I did not hear their concerns. In fact, I was stubborn and the only way I knew how to deal with myself was through work.

In February 1977, Kim Gie, the man I had become close to at my last job tracked me down and showed up one day. Shortly after opening the club, he came in asking where I was. One of the girls called me and told me someone was there to see me. My heart was nervous at the thought of my mother because in the world, there wasn't anyone looking for me except my mother. I dropped what I was doing and went into the club. Again, I was stunned at the sight of this man and he smiled at me, but I could not smile or say a word. He approached me slowly, grabbed my shoulders and said, "I have been looking all over for you. Why didn't you tell me?" Finally, I calmed down myself and said to him, "Please come and sit here."

We sat at a table and talked for a while. I hugged him and I never let go of him again, but I did not show my feelings to this man. He ordered drinks and I studied his face. To me, he seemed to have lost weight. He asked me to meet him after work and gave me his room number. I went to him after midnight. When I arrived, he took me into his arms and held me tightly. I sensed that something was very wrong and asked him if there was anything I could do. He shook his head and started talking about how little time he had left before he would die. I was stricken by this sad news. I asked him about what was going on with his health. He said that he had T.B. and it had finally took over his body and he was getting weak every day. I did remember he was carrying x-ray film once, but I did not ask what that was.

Here we were again; his sickness was the same as my dad and he was dying similarly like my dad. At last, he finally came clean and told me the truth about himself. I was not surprised that he had a wife and children. Being a working girl, I did not care if he had family. I cared for him right then. I could not give him a new life ,but whatever the moment I wanted to spend with him as long as I could remember. He told me one last time, "I want you to leave the club, and I want you to come to Seoul with me." I asked him what I would do for a living and he said he knew many places. He would find something better suited for me. I did not respond; in my heart I wanted go with him to Seoul, but I could not. The next morning we parted and he returned to Seoul.

In the spring of 1978, I was tired of being man-handled by so many Korean men. I was just living aimlessly with no hope or direction for the future. I decided to return to Seoul to seek a better future. I thought the big city was still better for me, whatever I decided to do. On the train ride, I thought a lot about Mrs. Park, if there was something she could do for me, if she still thought about me. As soon as I arrived in Seoul, I dialed her home. Her phone number was the same and she answered the phone. I said, "Mom," she said, "Kyong Mi." She seemed surprised to hear from me. She had forgiven me. She had not lost her tenderness toward understanding human misery. She was catching up with me about her family and told me that her daughter got married and had a son. She also told me that Won Ae would love to see me. Wherever I was, these two people were always in my heart, and I was thinking about seeing her daughter again. I was so happy I could have cried. Mrs. Park told me to come over, and when I got there, dinner was waiting for me. As we ate, she told me how grown up I seemed. She called her daughter and told her we would be there after dinner. When we arrived at her daughter's home I looked around outside. Her house was lit up like some kind of a happy event in her family. Mrs. Park approached the metal gate and buzzed the doorbell. The chauffeur opened the door politely and invited us in. We got into the living room; Won Ae was waiting and she was thrilled to see me and gave me a hug. I was her old friend. A friend she had never forgotten. Her husband came downstairs and said, "I have heard a lot about you from time to time." He also showed me politeness and I felt that I was home. We all sat in the living room and caught up on what we had lost in time. Won Ae and her husband were a wealthy couple. They would hire me if I wanted to be a live-in maid. Without a second thought I said, yes, and I would be delighted. That same night I moved in, and I thanked them for the job. I was nervous because I did not have enough money.

A couple of months went by, and I began to understand the daily routine and each day become easier to work. I had not worked a maid's job for a while, so I was tired. I was up and down stairs almost all day long, and my body was retaining water. I was swollen like a balloon. Often, I remembered my relationship with Won Ae when she was a college student. My memory kept traveling to the past and I had no idea how much she had changed in the years we were apart. I was looking for our old relationship as sisters. Won Ae was now the woman of the house with a husband, child, mother-in-law, and brother-in law. I felt left out and I couldn't understand about how the relationship formed and it wasn't mutual. The wall around my heart kept building, and in this household of people, I was lonely and treated as a stranger. Since I didn't want to lose my connection with Mrs. Park, I stayed with Won Ae for about a year. I thought I could do the demanding work of being a maid again, but I was wrong. I developed vertigo which made working difficult and as I would get dizzy and would fall down the stairs numerous times a day. I explained to Won Ae that I would have to leave. She asked me to stay and invited me to one of her Bible study groups held at her home. Won Ae introduced me to the group through my life story. They prayed for me, but at the time I didn't believe in anything and wondered why I was there. I felt nothing and I had to leave. No matter how much she wanted me to stay, I had to pack up.

I was on the road again without a destination in sight. I looked in the paper again and ended up finding a job as a guide for the Japanese. I knew just enough Japanese to get by. I was able to travel and I met a lot of very nice Japanese men. I had many Japanese clients who treated me very well and they were generous which allowed me to live well. I still did not have a home, but many clients continued to come to see me from Japan, and I would stay with them in a hotel until they left Korea. Even though I was doing well, I felt like I was drawing deeper into the abyss, and every time I came up for air, there was a tremendous weight that kept pulling me back under and I could not get anywhere. I handled the mental anguish and the physical abuse of the past, and yet, I did not know how strong I was. That weight on my shoulders and in my chest, everything I had experienced in my life made me who I was, but I could not hold my head up high. I was never enough and I still wanted to better for myself, but where would I go from here? I needed something that would give my life meaning and I wanted to hold on to something that would last forever. I was forever trying to get out of woven messes, but there was always an obstacle in my way. At times I thought that dying was easier than living.

Five

In the fall of 1979, I traveled to Young Ju Gol, north of Seoul, near the parallel. It was a small town and everyone knew each household and I found a job as a masseuse. It was located in a hotel with six rooms dedicated to massage and Turkish baths. When a client came in, they were assigned to a girl who would bathe them and give a massage. This turned out to be a horrible place to work. Even though I could choose which man to stay with, most of them were abusive Korean soldiers. However, I also met some influential people such as doctors, lawyers, and law enforcers. No one I met here was important to me. I felt doomed. I was a beautiful creature who was being crushed under the feet of men.

I was struggling with trying to find way out of the place; however, my life changed on the morning of June 24, 1979. It was the morning I had a touch of vertigo and I stepped down to a hallway window. I opened the window and looked out on the church on the hill. The church on the hill always made me feel welcome, but I never went up that hill. And sometimes, I heard the sound of the bell on Sunday morning, and the sound of the bell gripped my heart and it was calling me to come. While I was enjoying the sun and the church, suddenly, I heard footsteps coming upstairs. It was the morning of my turn to work. I asked the man if he was there for a massage. He said no, that he was looking for a girl named Myung Ja. I told him where she was. He was an impressively good-looking man. He was young and his skin color was darker than that of most

Koreans. He had big brown eyes, dark, long, curly hair and he was wearing long sleeves even though it was summer.

On the same day in the afternoon, I saw him again with Myung Ja. They asked me if I was interested in going fishing with them. I thought to myself that I had never been fishing before and it could be a new and different experience. I told them I wanted to go, and they told me that the three of us would leave late in the afternoon. I had no question in my mind about this trip. However, my heart felt such an excitement but I did not know there would be such a price to pay; and I had not even dreamed about what kind of man he was. He was my first and last boyfriend from Korea and his name was Sung Ha Jo.

In the late afternoon, around four o'clock, Sung Ha came to pick me up at work. He wanted me to go with him downtown to pick up fishing gear, camping equipment and fish bait. He drove his white car and on the way downtown we stopped at his home and he introduced me to his sister-in-law who lived a couple of blocks away from where I was working. She had a husband and also living with her were two children and Sung Ha. I did not see her husband then, but met him several hours later at the fishing site. It was a brief meeting, but I thought about that family on the way downtown. We arrived at the club and he explained to me that it was his work place. His work place was dark with whole walls with mirrors and in the middle of the ceiling there was a dangling light. There was a waxed floor that was shiny and slippery. I was busy looking around the place, and he introduced me to several of his friends. All of his friends shook my hand and said to me, "Where have you been hiding?" Sung Ha told them to be respectable because I was not like Myung Ja, besides, I did not know how to dance either.

Sung Ha was very sociable, as were all of his friends. Sung Ha and his brother were both well known ballroom dancers in Korea and their circle of friends were dancers too. We got back into the car and to continued to drive through the downtown. I was very quiet in the car and I said to him, "You must be a very nice and popular person." Sung Ha asked me, "Why I don't you have any friends?" Without hesitation I said to him, "No." For some reason, I never thought about anyone as my friends and someone I worked with was not my friend. I only knew that my real friends would be who I grew up with. He paused. Maybe he did not know what else he could say to me. Often, his eyes held questions in them when he looked at me. Each time I kept turning my head toward him, and I sensed that something was happening between us very quickly, but I was not aware of it as we drove. A connection between us was building without the words and I did not know what the connection between Sung Ha and I was. I ignored my feelings. He was a gentle man and treated me like a queen. In my life, prior to this man I had no idea what was like to be with a man.

Our next stop was the bait shop. He purchased a bucket of minnows, several containers of worms, and a few packages of fishing hooks. It was the first time I saw the fishing hooks and even minnows. He explained to me what the things in the shop were and what to use for different fishing. Our shopping was complete, but he had one more stop to make at a place where his brother was waiting for him. Sung Ha stopped at the bar to talk to his brother and returned to the car less then five minutes later. He'd said, "Let's go now." We were driving on the freeway. I felt something was different about the field. I knew I had seen this place almost every day but I never felt this field made me like a whole different person inside. *Maybe it's because Sung Ha is with me*, I'd thought. We returned to my place of employment, and as we drove, I studied his face. Occasionally, he stretched his hand out to me, and held my hand. I was just quiet, even though my heart started beating faster. For the first time in my life, I felt something tingling within my heart. I wished I could touch him, be with him, but I couldn't because he was another woman's man. At that moment, I was wearing a mask so no one could detect what was in my heart.

When we arrived, he opened my door and said, "I will be back in a few minutes. I must go home to change and get the rest of the gear, then we will go to the lake." I rushed upstairs and called Myung Ja, whom everyone at work called Miss Kwang. I packed a blanket, sweater, toothbrush etc. Then I called out to Myung Ja, "Let's go. Come on! Sung Ha is waiting downstairs!" Miss Kwang did not respond, so I went to her room. When I got there, she was taking a nap. She had been drinking. I woke her up. She was still in a haze. She finally dragged herself downstairs and Sung Ha opened the back door of his car for her. Sung Ha said to me, "You sit on the front seat with me." I did exactly what he said. Sung Ha told Myung Ja his brother would join us later, and both of them were talking, but I did not respond. My girlfriend was drinking and the music was playing very loud, so I could not hear what he was saying. We drove for about two hours and we finally arrived at a quiet place on the water. The lake was cool and calm, and the sun was setting to the west. Sung Ha started setting up the tent where the three of us would be sleeping, and I was lending him extra help. Sung Ha was impressed by my action. As he was doing this, his brother and the other girl whom I worked with arrived. They were planning on going home so they had no tent to set up. Myung Ja was still out of it, so I set up the campfire, knowing I would be doing the cooking.

Myung Ja remained in the tent while the four of us fished about 20 feet away from the tent downhill. I caught the first fish, and I was very excited because I had never fished before. Sung Ha ran down to where I was and grabbed my pole and landed the fish. We fished for a few hours and when it started getting dark, I gutted and cleaned the fish and cooked them for everyone's dinner. The brothers had a few beers and the other girl didn't like getting her hands dirty, so she sat with the brothers. Myung Ja finally woke up in time for dinner. We all sat around the fire and ate. They were all impressed with my cooking. Afterwards, I cleaned up and Sung Ha jumped in to help and so I let him. The brothers decided to do some night fishing and Myung Ja decided to retire. Sung Ha was fishing about 15 feet away from me when I caught another fish. He came to my aid and then said he needed to talk to me. I recast and sat down and he sat down behind me. He hugged me from behind and said into my ear, "Myung Ja and I got drunk last night. I woke up beside her, but I want you to know nothing happened between us." He continued stating that his best friend was her boyfriend and that he would be here in the morning. We caught more fish in the remaining hours until dark, and fish went into the cooler for the next day.

It was late night at the lake. There were four of us and more beer bottles went around. Everyone's voices carried over a quiet lake and I was amused by the way they carried their conversations. Around 11:30 p.m., Sung Ha's brother left with the other girl. In the light of the full moon, the sky was crispy clear, as the darker sky was dotted with shining sparkles. Sung Ha asked me how I felt about walking with him around the lake. I accepted his invitation. As we walked in the moonlight, he asked me if I was cold, as the wind had picked up. I'd told him I felt a little chilled, so he took off his jacket and put it over my shoulders and drew me closer to him. He kissed me softly on my cheek and held me like I was a breakable object. I felt warm and safe in his arms. I had never felt this way with anyone else. In fact, he was the first man ever. As we walked, I leaned my head on his chest. He stopped and kissed me on my lips. This was the first romantic kiss I had ever experienced. I got goosebumps and was extremely happy. My heart was filled with something I could not explain. The night grew darker; the stars were hanging low and the full moon lit the sky. How could I ever forget that night? Whatever we had just shared, I took very seriously. I thought about maybe it was love at first sight.

When we returned to the tent, Myung Ja was sitting outside the tent and smoking. She asked us where we had been. Sung Ha told her we had been for a walk around the lake. She seemed upset but didn't say anything. Sung Ha said he was tired and was going to bed. He asked me to come with him. I followed him into the tent and he turned to ask Myung Ja if she was coming. She'd snapped, "In a minute." Sung Ha told me to sleep at the left side of the tent and he slept in the middle. I fell asleep right away but my mind was actively thinking over and over what happened while we were walking. It was a wonderful feeling being held by him. With him, I was Kay, not Kyong Mi. He comforted me like I was in the warm, fluffy blanket. I kept thinking to myself, *Why would this man want to be with me?* Since I was sleeping lightly, I could feel Sung Ha moving closer to me and I kept scooting closer to the wall away from him. Eventually he turned on his side and threw his arm over me. I let him and drifted off.

In the morning, when Sung Ha and I woke up, he kissed me and said, "Good morning." He seemed happy. He looked to the right and noticed Myung Ja was gone. He rushed out of the tent to look for her. He found her in his car asleep in the back seat. He woke her up and asked, "Why are you here?" She told him that when she came in to sleep, "You and Kay looked too cozy and I did not want to interrupt anything!" She was very sarcastic. While this was happening, I was setting up to make breakfast. Her voice carried over the quiet morning lake and I could hear what was going on. However, I pretended that I didn't hear anything and I didn't care how she felt.

I continued to make coffee and breakfast for us. Just as breakfast was ready to be served, Sung Ha's best friend, Myung Ja's boyfriend, arrived. Myung Ja's boyfriend was upbeat and greeted her affectionately. After Sung Ha introduced us, we seemed comfortable with each other right away. After breakfast, as I was cleaning up, they sat around drinking Johnny Walker Red. The three of us, Sung Ha, his friend and I fished, but we did not catch anything that morning. Later that morning Sung Ha told his friend to take Myung Ja home and that he would pack up and bring me home. Myung Ja had a fit, but ended up going home with her boyfriend. I breathed a sigh of relief once she was gone. Sung Ha was shaking his head but said to me that we would stay another day if that was alright with me. Naturally, I said, "Fine." Just being there with him and laughing was enough for me. We fished until late that night, then we decided to pack up and return home. Sung Ha told me on the way back home that he wanted to see me seriously. He also told me Myung Ja was only paying him for dance lessons. He told me not to worry about her. I knew she had a big drinking problem, but I did not know what kind of person she was. She possessed aggressive behavior and a terrible temper which none of her friends wanted to deal with. It was perfect timing for Sung Ha because I was a young, very pretty person, my personality like a lamb. I also had a sense of how to please him. Finally, he resolved his sore thumb when he got rid of her, but I had to deal with rest of my girlfriend's awful behaviors.

The following night, Myung Ja showed up drunk, pounding at my door. I was afraid to open it. She screamed through the door at me. She accused me of stealing her boyfriend. The older lady from next door came out and asked Myung Ja to quiet down. She took her into her room to try to calm her down. I could hear through the walls that Myung Ja was being told that I was not at fault here and Myung Ja should be talking to Sung Ha. The old woman called Sung Ha and let him know what was happening and told him to come over. When Sung Ha arrived, I did not open my door for him. I told him the fishing trip was a big mistake and I never wanted to see him again. Myung Ja and my neighbor were present when I said this. I closed my door on all of them.

A few weeks passed without incident. About the middle of July, I had a feeling that I would see Sung Ha again. Sure enough, one evening as the sun was setting, I heard familiar footsteps coming up the stairs. I opened my door and Sung Ha was standing there. He smiled at me and was ready to enter my room, but I called for the older woman next door to come. She came over and brought him in with her. He thanked her and I didn't say anything. My older neighbor told him that if he wanted to continue a relationship with me that he must set things straight with Myung Ja, otherwise I would be in danger. Sung Ha promised he would take care of the matter and she returned to her room.

Once we were alone, Sung Ha told me how much he missed me. He wanted to spend the night with me but I asked him to leave. I realized that Myung Ja and I had drifted apart and the other girls also. I just could not bear the awful feeling towards all people, the way they looked at me. I became a man snatcher. That night he refused to go home, so I ended up letting him stay with me. I told him how uneasy I felt because Myung Ja was still living down the hall. He kept telling me not to worry. He was very gentle to me that night as we made love for the first time. For the first time in my life, I wanted him at first sight at the lake, in the tent. He kept assuring me he would be here every night with me to protect me from Myung Ja's harassment. He did live up to his promise.

One night before Sung Ha arrived, Myung Ja was drunk and broke down my door. She had a broken bottle in her hand and threatened to cut me. My neighbor heard the commotion and called Sung Ha. The owner of the work place heard the commotion and ran upstairs before Sung Ha arrived. The owner grabbed her arm tightly and he started yelling at her about how awful her behavior was. The owner spoke to her like a father talking to a daughter, that her idiotic senseless act towards a fellow friend was not acceptable at his work place; for this reason, she'd better behave and leave me alone because for every action, there would be a consequence.

Once Sung Ha arrived, both of them took Myung Ja into the room and at last, the place was finally quiet. After this incident, she steered clear of me and so often, I only got dirty looks. Shortly after this incident, Myung Ja apologized to me because she finally realized that Sung Ha was not meant to be with her. As a result, my life was running smoothly with Sung Ha. He was stopping by as often as he could and I had a chance to know him a little better. When he was with me, we talked mostly about his family and through our conversations, I discovered that he was also had a dark side to his life story. Sung Ha lost his mom and dad when he was very young, but he had two older brothers and two sisters who took care of him. Eventually, I met his family one person at a time, and they liked to question me very much, but I did not have much story to tell them. One thing they knew was that I did not have a family, and I did not have a friend. Sometimes, Sung Ha's family invited me to go fishing and I would be thrilled to go. I loved to spend the time together for any occasions where I cooked with his sisters, especially a few holiday meals. They made me welcome and feel like part of a family I never had.

The weather was getting colder and I knew my birthday was getting closer. What a marvelous fishing trip we had, and being with Sung Ha, my life was fun and unpredictable because I really did not know one day to the next. I was 21 years old and he was 25 years old. We had been going out for almost five months. He never asked me when my birthday was, but something was waiting for me, and yet, I would not even imagine what that surprise was. When he showed up at my door and asked me to open it, there he was, wearing a black long winter coat and holding a heart shaped white box. He'd handed it to me proudly, saying, "Open it." I lifted the lid and I was in shock. It was a white, heart-shaped, beautifully decorated birthday cake. It was the first time I ever received my birthday present in my entire life. Tears of joy rolled down my cheeks. There was no birthday song, but everyone clapped and seemed happy for me. At this point in our relationship, I would do anything for this man, and I did. I had lived a solitary life for a very long time and Sung Ha was the only hope of light that made me feel alive. I was happy, like some kind of magic spell was over me and I did not want to wake up from it.

It was spring of 1980, and I did not hear from Sung Ha for about a week. I was concerned, worried about him. There were all kinds of negative thoughts racing through my head like train tracks. I anxiously waited for him to contact me. The days went by and there was no sign of Sung Ha. I waited long enough and I decided to go his brother's home. It was a dreary spring day and this would be the first time I ever visited where he lived. When I arrived, his sister-in-law let me in and she said, "My brother-in-law is very ill." She pointed to where Sung Ha was. I knocked at the bedroom door and no one answered so I opened the door. Sung Ha was laying covered up on his bedroll. His face looked drawn, his eyes were sunken and his color was unnaturally pale. My heart ached when I saw him this way. He seemed surprised to see me, and he reached out his hand to touch me. I sat by him and held his hand. Then I asked him how long had he been this way. He said about a week. I asked him if he had seen a doctor and he said no, that he would be fine, but I insisted that he go to see my doctor and that I would pay for it. I sat with him for a few hours and I told him that I would stop at the doctor's office to let him know to expect Sung Ha's visit.

Late afternoon that day, the doctor called me regarding Sung Ha's diagnosis. The doctor said that Sung Ha had seen him and been given an acupuncture treatment, including natural remedies. Consequently, the most important news was that he had a bad liver. The doctor also said that he had to watch his drinking and the frequency of intercourse with me, or anyone else. I thanked the doctor and asked him if he would continue to receive his treatment and I would be picking up the bills.

His treatment lasted for about four or five months, and in the meantime I worked very hard because I had to pay his doctors visits and treatments. Above all, I took some time off from work and I stayed with him because I wanted to make natural remedies for him. The ingredients of natural remedies were the mixtures of tree barks, roots, dry plants and the dry antlers of deer. I believed that when it slow boils in the crock pot, I put my pure energy into it and he would heal faster. As a result, he gained his strength and he got better before the winter arrived. I was planning on giving him his birthday present but it did not happen the way I expected it to. I felt a little guilt, but I did not want to think about my guilt. In spite of what was going on in my heart, Sung Ha wanted to move out of his brother's house because his nephews were getting older and they needed separate rooms. It was very odd that he even talked to me about it but I agreed to help him. He found an apartment where he could be working and told me how much it would cost. I gave him money to move and took care of the rest of his household needs. I took financial burden for him; I thought it would be worth it because I loved Sung Ha endlessly. In truth, I never knew how to put myself first and it did not matter how hard I had to work in order to support Sung Ha. I knew I could never be his wife, but while that might have been true, I was acting as his wife. The time I had with Sung Ha was the most important part of my life because it was a part of me awakened by him. But he also pulled me into the darkness.

During this time, my clientele was made up of influential people. These people were detectives, doctors, lawyers, judges and the mayor of the city. I made pretty good money as well as plenty of good friends all over the area. All these clients were aware of my relationship with Sung Ha and were free with their advice to me, but I pretended not to hear their advice. It was one summer day in 1981 Sung Ha came to see me at my work. He wished he had a diamond ring like other dancers wore. I was afraid of losing him; therefore, I offered to buy the ring for him. I knew this ring would cost me years of work to pay for it, but I managed to get a ring for him as well as an expensive watch. I felt sure he would stay with me because of the gifts I gave him. I never asked how he spent the money he made. He was paid to be a dancing partner and escort for women, therefore, he always dressed in expensive clothing and was well groomed. There were women beside him constantly. Yet, I trusted him because maybe I was not the person to ask questions about his work or relationship with any other women. I did not know what I was entitled to. I was his girlfriend who had given all that she was.

After he received the jewelry, he seemed to drift away from me slowly. I was being naïve. I didn't notice right away and it took me a little while to become aware of our relationship. Without knowing what a relationship should be, I still went to his apartment once a week. When I visited him, he was not in his apartment. When I was in his room I cooked, cleaned and did his laundry. I pretended that I didn't notice his distance, but also during this time his family and I became close. I feel they thought Sung Ha and I would eventually be together, so they treated me like a family member.

In the winter of that year, I went to his house as usual to bring him what I cooked. When I got there, I let myself in and discovered Sung Ha in bed with another person. I dropped the container of food and rushed out the door and stood with my arms crossed in the alley near his front door. Sung Ha had gotten dressed to go somewhere and he opened the door. He saw me standing in front of his door and told me to go home and he would stop by later that day. I noticed a woman behind him, so I knew then he was seeing someone else. She was of small build, short hair and she looked very intelligent. My heart was broken terribly; I could not say any word to him even if he was with another woman. I'd rented an apartment for him because he wanted to be free and I gave all I could to support him. I cried all the way to my place on the bus. I did not have anyone to talk to and my heart was hidden from my co-workers because I did not want anyone to know about what was happening. That same night, he came over my place and said I should never to come over to his apartment again. I was devastated and I knew I was losing his presence and he moved away shortly after that visit. I did not know where he moved to.

For a while, I tried contacting him at his club, but they would not tell me where he was. Sung Ha probably thought that I would eventually give up trying to contact him, which I did for about six months. However, I still ran into his family members who remained friendly to me, but they said Sung Ha didn't visit there often anymore.

During those six months, I just worked and tried to forget about him, however, my co-workers would come back with stories about seeing Sung Ha and they had danced with him. I didn't know whether they were trying to hurt me or not. I also decided at that time to take dance lessons so I could at least see him once in a while. When he would see me at the club, he avoided me. On the other hand, I was obsessed with him and as a result, I did not work as much as when Sung Ha was around. Furthermore, during this time, my top priorities were dancing and drinking. I was still paying Sung Ha's debt. I had nowhere to turn and no one to confide in. I felt totally alone and was at the lowest point in my life without feeling I had to kill myself. Yet, it was just my stupid thoughts and I could not do that again. Whatever the reason, I was still hanging onto him for some reason. In this devastation, nothing any worst than more bad news from my mother. I took the deep plunge into the darkness again without knowing how to get out of the woven mess.

Six

Thinking things could not get any worse, I received a call from my sister, Kyong Hie, at the beginning of July 1982 in An Sung, where my mother was. I did not know how she had gotten hold of my phone number, but I did not ask her. I had not seen my sister for about ten years. The last time I saw my mother was the fall of 1976 and since then, I refused to see her. I did not think anyone would contact me in my workplace. I had isolated myself from my family and my sister Kyong Hie, having not thought about her for a long time. Yet there she was. I did not even know what she looked like, but on the phone it sounded like my sister. She told me that Mom had been very ill and she was asking for me to come to see her. It was not a hard decision for me to get away. In fact, this trip would distance me from my problems with Sung Ha.

When I arrived, Kyong Hie was sitting with my dying mother and told me how upset she was with me. She said she had come to visit her and ended up taking care of this woman ever since. She told me it was my turn to take care of her, and she packed up and left. I knew my sister was a very cold person, but I never thought that she would actually show her true self to me and in front of her own mother. I knew I had to pull myself together in order to get through. How awful life was between Mom and me, but it wasn't the right time for me to think about it. In this awful situation, the most important issue was that I must take care of her, make her as comfortable as possible. *Finally, two of us in this small room without her companion who should have been taking care of her, but instead I had to take care of her until the last day of her life,* I thought. She looked very thin and frail, but also, she had an abnormal growth on the side of her neck. The growth was the size of a melon, and it interfered with her throat. She looked like a bag of bones lying on the floor without any support from anyone. I stood there in shock and was motionless. I heard Mom said, "Kyong Mi, come sit." I sat next to her and I looked at her closely without any word. I knew she was happy to see me, and maybe, she knew I would take care of her without complaint. She began to talk to me and she sounded like a child tattling on another child while her story continued. My sister refused to feed her because she would vomit everything that she had been consuming.

Obviously, my sister did not want to clean up the mess. I assured her that I would make sure she was fed and cleaned up. The first thing I did was give her a bath. Her skin was mostly dry flakes and the only thing left over on her body was just heavy bones. At first, it was very hard even though she was thin I had to carry her to the shower in the kitchen floor in order to give her the bath. When her bathing was done, I made some soup for her. As I put a spoon full of liquid in her mouth, I noticed her eyes were filled with tears. I asked her why she was crying and she said that sometimes, she wet the bed because my sister could not hear her mother's call. I knew my sister had ignored mother's calling. I took care of her best as I could and comforted her with all my strength. I thought that it was the only time I could take good care of her and showed her that I was still her daughter, even if she did wrong to me when I was a little girl. She abused me and neglected me every way she could but I could not pay back to her what she did. I was listening to what my mother said and I had tears because it was the saddest moment to see how she was dying. I felt that no one deserved to be dying like that. *I thought, if my mother had money, would my sister have treated her the way she did?* I knew I would not see her ever again when I left.

Some days, when she was soundly sleeping, I cried in the kitchen or in the attic not because she was dying but because I was going to lose shadows of my mother.

While I was there, I asked my mom about her boyfriend. She told me he was married and where he lived. The reason I asked her because I was angry at him, and I just wanted to know what he looked like. When I saw him I asked why he had to leave my mom: was it because she no longer had use of her body or he did not want the responsibility? I found his home and the company he owned in the marketplace.

I went inside and asked for him and a woman appeared. She must have been his wife and called him. He knew who I was. I confronted him and I could have asked him why he had to leave ,but I did not. I realized it was not my place to say anything and I did not know him either. Instead, I asked him to help me to make funeral arrangements. He'd said he would like to help financially, but the economy had been very slow and he was having a problem in his business. He would be unable to help but he would find a funeral home. I thanked him and left. On the way home, I tasted the bitterness in my mouth and thought, *What kind of man would leave a woman he once cared for, just in time for her to die?* I was 25 years old but I could not understand men. As I was walking the marketplace I firmly promised myself that I would never die like my mother. At least, I will save money for own funeral while I was still young. As I was thinking about my mother, I had a knot tightening in my heart and I did not know what went wrong in her life. She had five daughters but I was the only one took care of everything as a child and now. Mother was not an old woman but what made her easily give up on her life? I realized that something was not right in her life. As my thought produced more and more about her life, I was getting angrier and I had to shut my mind and continue to stroll home.

When I returned home, Mom had been awakened and she asked

me where I had been. I said that I had been at the market. I did not want her to know where I had been and whom I had met. By evening, I decided to ask my mother what had been bothering me my whole life. So I asked her," Mom, why did you hurt me when I was little?" Her answer was, "I am sorry." That was it. I thought, *How simple.* She had no idea how long I had carried those pains and wanted to hear more explanations but I couldn't ask her any more. I was in her attic, smoking, and I'd thought about what she just said and thought to myself, *That isn't good enough.* I needed to hear more explanations but she would not say anything else and closed her eyes. I knew she wanted to say more but she did not know how to tell me the details or she maybe she did not know why either.

I had been with my mom almost two and a half weeks, and I began to worry about my work. I told my mom that I had to return to work and I would be leaving within in a few days. I saw her eyes were saddened by my news. She definitely did not want my sister back, so I had to make arrangements with a neighbor of hers. I told the neighbor that if an emergency arose, she must call my sister but otherwise, I would be returning very soon. The neighbor and I got to know each other a little better and she told me about a lot of things that had happened before my sister came to visit my mom. Her neighbor had been helping my mom when my sister was not around. Her neighbor explained that she had been cutting Mom's hair and her church congregation had been visiting Mom almost everyday. Thus, the owner of Mom's place was not a good person because when my mom got sicker, the owner's family packed up and left. The owner yelled at Mom because rent was behind and a dying person in her house might bring in bad luck. I thanked the neighbor for her generosity and asked her to continue looking out for a while longer. I told the neighbor that I would be back as soon as money was in my hands. I hated the place but what else I could I do to make her better? The only solution was to wait for Mom's life to end, and hope that it was without any worse pain.

Finally, Mother spoke her last words to me. She said to please bring back money when I returned and she did not have a lot of time left for her funeral. In addition, she requested about where I could spread her ashes. There were specific details about what I should do if I had a chance to see her last breath. She said that I should touch her body because she would take away my illness by touching her. I had a feeling that she wouldn't last a week. It was July 21, 1982. I told Mom that her neighbor would be taking care of her for a few days, and my sister would be there for her until my return. I felt that it was a point of no return to see Mom again, and on my way on the bus my tears rolled down like the summer monsoon.

When I returned to Seoul, I visited Mrs. Park, and asked her to help me with money for my mother's funeral expense. I would pay her back after the funeral but her answer was "NO." She did not lend me money but fed me and told me to visit any time. She knew I needed her a little longer for some reason. Late that night I arrived at work. My co-worker asked about my mom and I broke down in tears as I told them she was dying.

One of my co-workers said that she ran into Sung Ha and told him where I was and the difficult situation I had faced with my mother. She said that Sung Ha had no reaction to this news and her impression of him was that he did not care. When I heard this, I was fuming mad and I wanted revenge. I did not know how to get revenge but I promised myself I would. I had previously found out that Sung Ha had been in trouble with the law and he was on probation, and the probation would end in a couple of months. I knew that if he got into trouble now he would really pay. My anger fueled me hotter than any other time ever before and I talked with my co-worker, the older friend next door. I knew she could give me wise advice. I talked to her and her answer was if I was planning on doing something really bad, I should talk with one of my clients about what was going on my life. So I decided to hatch a plot to get him in trouble; however, I still didn't know where he lived. The days went by faster and I worked as many clients as possible. I was carrying a broken heart and a burden. The only way get rid of both was that I had to do something.

It had been a week after returning from my mom, and I had a dream about a huge bathhouse in the city, north from where I worked. *In the middle of the bathhouse, there was a huge tub filled with clear water, and suddenly the water churned into violent waves. My dream was darker shades of color and I was a little scared. I left the bathhouse and walked up the hills and it was early in the morning. There were no streetlights but I was able to see several stores along the street. As I wandered around the area I woke up. Later that morning, a boyfriend of one of the co-workers told me that he had seen Sung Ha in front of a bathhouse in the city of Moon San. It was connected to my dream and I knew the exact location. Sung Ha had been going to the same bathhouse like everyone else, and he may have dropped his laundry to the store around the area I had seen in my dream.* All day, I thought about the dream I had the night before, and that night I had another dream. *My dream was about my mother who confirmed my feeling that she was going to die at the end of July, but it was just a hunch. The dream was about me walking up a mountain whose trees had been destroyed by fire. On the barren brown ground, I could see the trees and the grasses were burned. The weather was sunny but humid. I was wearing a white Korean dress without shoes on my feet. I felt that the debris poking under my feet was like a thorn bush but I still could walk up a steep mountainside. Out of nowhere, there was a large black Doberman that followed me and bit my right heel before I woke up.* My body was drenched and thirsty when I realized it was just another stupid dream. My dream was haunting me for some reason but I trusted that it was a warning.

I had awful dreams two nights in row, and I desperately needed money for cremating my mother. After a couple of days of thought, I decided to find Sung Ha. Surely, I knew the location of the bathhouse where someone else saw him and the fact that he took his shirts to the cleaners. I was in the city of Moon San, and I started my investigation. The first cleaners I went into happened to be the one where he took his clothes, and with this information, I went to see my detective client in the police station. I explained my story to him about Mom and how I needed money desperately. Besides, I had given a gift to Sung Ha, and he was serving three years of probation. I asked my detective friend to find Sung Ha and see if he could get money from him for me. The detective friend had listened quietly and said, "I told you before but you did not listen to what I said." He said to me, "Do not worry. I will find him and get what you want." The next thing I knew I heard Sung Ha's voice in the station. My heart was beating faster and I was scared because I did something awful and I already regretted what I had done. I was in the next room from where Sung Ha was. I overheard the detective telling Sung Ha that he had no right to take from someone as poor as Kay.

The detective demanded that Sung Ha should give back the jewelry and anything else that she had given him. Sung Ha made a phone call from the station, and told the person on the other line what to pack up and put in a taxi and send to the police station. Otherwise, he would not be let go until it arrived. I was standing in the dark thinking, *How could he do this to me and why? What did I do wrong except give myself to him completely?*

That was the end of my sad love story. In my mind, there were many questions that had been left unanswered and I had to move on. After the taxi arrived, the detective asked me to come into the office and told us to resolve whatever was left undone. I saw Sung Ha's face since he left within several months. He looked like a ghost, and filled with pain. I'd had my revenge. I had cried for his love, but he did not return to me. I asked for help when I needed him desperately, but he rejected me. I wanted him to be just a good friend but he also refused. I was looking at him, under the room where most people do not want to be in. At that moment, I felt I was in the right and he got what he deserved. I couldn't cry. I had righteous anger toward him. The detective left us in the room together and Sung Ha said to me, "I am sorry, but you should not have done this." Then he gave me the diamond ring that I had bought for him the second year we were together for his birthday. He said, "You had your revenge. I hope you live a great life." It was his spiteful curse but I did not make any assumption, and I said to him, "Thank you and I hope you do, too." We had just about ended our conversation when the detective came into the office and said, "You can go home now." The detective walked with me in the hallway and said, "This is your last time and do not contact each other ever again." It was the first time and the one last time Sung Ha called me by my real name, Kyong Mi, and he said to me again, "I hope you will have a great life." As I stepped out of the station I said, "You, too." It was July 30, 1982, after midnight. On the way home, I looked out the window and recalled my memory of what I had shared with Sung Ha at the lake. How innocent and happy we were then, but at this moment, my heart was terribly broken and filled with anger. I committed a terrible crime that I couldn't forgive myself for against the person I had loved very much once upon a time. I may be responsible for wrongdoing to Sung Ha and I will face consequences in the future, and a part of me was already asking for forgiveness.

The taxi arrived at the place I needed to sell what I had. It was almost after 1:00 a.m. and the store was still open. I needed money right away. Instead of waiting for the daylight, I took things to the grocery store. The owner who owned the grocery store said she may buy it. I hoped that she would give me money; she might buy and be better than the pawn shop if I explained what was going on with my mom; she might understand. I took all the things returned from Sung Ha to the woman who owned the grocery store downstairs from where I worked. I was right. I explained my situations with Sung Ha and my mother. I had enough money to go visit my dying mother as quickly as possible.

Seven

It was the bright morning of July 31,1982; I woke up around 7:00 a.m. and cleaned my room and the hallway. It was about 9:00 a.m. when someone told me I had a phone call. I rushed downstairs and the owner told me it was my sister. She told me Mom was dying and asked me to come right away. I threw a few things in an overnight bag and left. On the way home on the bus, I prayed that she would stay alive until I got there, but after arriving around 1:00 p.m., my mom was already gone. The day was extremely hot and I had a ten-minute walk to my mom's. As I turned the corner to go into Mom's home, my grandmother was squatting outside and having a smoke in order to hide herself from the burning afternoon sun. I said "Hi" as I passed her and went into the room. Once inside, I saw my sister, Kyong Hie, and my aunt. I had not seen my aunt for sometime and she looked much older than how I remembered. My aunt seemed surprised to see me and mourned out loud. It was Korean custom that everyone should let out mourning to the firstborn and that was what my aunt did. My grandmother and aunt left shortly after because my aunt had to work. She promised me they would be back the next day for the funeral.

My sister and I spoke briefly, than she left to run errands. This left me alone with my mom's body. Someone had put up a decorative folding screen around my mom. I wanted to see Mother's look but it was limited because Korean custom would not allow me to view her until someone from the morticians' office came. About a half-hour after my sister left, the mortician arrived. He told me to step back and he went behind the screen. He started talking to Mother while he was preparing her body for cremation. He finally folded back the screen and asked me to come to see her. When I came over to her, he was cleaning her from the waist up and asked me to watch. I noticed her stomach area was covered with purple bruises. He said, "She must have had a difficult life," and I responded, "Yes, she did." After awhile his filthy hands moved quickly over her face. The mortician washed Mother's face with a cloth. Suddenly, she opened her eyes and I gasped. He said that this woman must have a lasting regret and that's why her eyes opened. He closed her eyes gently, put rice in her mouth, and covered her lips with two coins. In Korean custom, for the spirit to travel from Earth to Heaven, it must have the coins in the mouth. The rice goes in the mouth so the spirit won't be hungry when it travels. The mortician dressed her in white and then placed her body in the coffin at last. The coffin was made of rough wood that the farmers used for packaging fruits. It was the cheapest thing I was able to purchase. Finally he put the folding screen back as preparation was complete and he quickly left the room as my sister returned.

We sat together for a moment and argued about something. She told me that I was not good enough to be her sister. I did not respond. I told her that I would go to take care of the paperwork at city hall. I just did not want to talk to her about my life and I did not know how to talk to her either. I wanted to avoid her the only way I knew. It was my behavior to run away from every situation instead of confronting the matters in life. When I returned from city hall, my sister left. It was around 6:00 p.m. and Mom's neighbor came to see me. She asked me how I was doing. She was concerned whether I had dinner and she brought me some food. I could not eat anything. My tongue was like rubber and anything it touched was tasteless, and I could not chew. When I chewed, I was chewing a spoonful of dirt in my mouth. The neighbor watched me for a few minutes then she went home. She came back with some soup so that at least I could swallow easily. She said to me, "Be strong, it will be alright." She continued. "Your mom is lucky woman because she has a daughter who knows what she is doing. I am so proud of you." The neighbor was talking to herself on and on. I drank a huge bowl of soup. It was cold and made of cucumber and the taste was sweet and sour. It boosted my lost appetite.

The night came. My body was exhausted from last night at the police station and at the store where I sold things from Sung Ha. I was sitting alone in this empty place. I was looking at the mirror. I was wearing a white dress, which most people wear when there are deceased in the family. I was weak. My face was white as a sheet of a paper. I must have closed my eyes, but something made me stay awake. I barely slept the night alone in my mom's house with a breathless corpse. It was early next morning, August 2, 1982. My grandmother, my aunt, her son, and my sister arrived. When the funeral bus arrived for my mother's body, the funeral director brought additional help. The coffin was carried out and placed in the back of the bus. Only three of us accompanied the coffin to the crematorium, my aunt, my sister and myself. The rest of the family stayed at my mother's home.

In the bus no one spoke; the silence was our guide. The trip to the crematorium was another stress even though I was just sitting in the seat. The road was winding with many curves. It seemed to me dying also requested the curves and many turns of the road, like human life. The road we had taken, uphill, downhill, and some areas were rocky. On the road for about an hour, we finally stopped at the quiet place of many trees, creeks, and singing birds welcoming us. The place should have been an inspiration to those who are there soul-searching and not the burning dead corpses. The place should have been for resting people like me because I was so tired by the time I arrived. The people at the crematorium took the coffin inside and I was asked to view the procedure. The people removed Mom's body from the coffin and placed her on the metal table that would take her through the fire. My aunt and sister were there to say their final goodbyes and then went to wait on the bus.

I, being first born, had to stay for the entire procedure. All I remember was watching her body being burned through the little glass window. The procedure would take about two hours and I could not stand for the entire time. I went outside and approached where my aunt was. At last, my aunt finally opened up to me for the first time. She said that she did not understand her sister until this day because no mother treated her own daughter the way she treated me, how cruel she was. My aunt mentioned that she remembered the many nights after my mom severely beat me when I would leave and return late. I would knock on my mom's door and when she would not answer, I would sit on the cement stairs and cry. I would then go to my aunt's to spend the night. She also told me that when my mom was pregnant with me, she shot her belly with heroin because she had so much pain from her ulcer. As I listened to my aunt, I thought about all the people who had rejected me and realized that even in my mother's womb, I must have felt rejection.

Just as our conversation ended, the man from the crematorium called me over to him. The table carrying the body was coming out the other side. On the table were bits of bone from the skull, shoulder bones, a couple of finger bones, a couple of ribs, pelvic bones and both femurs in the exact place where her body was laid. These pieces were taken to another area and smashed in a metal mortar and this was what they presented to me as my mom's ashes. While the man was smashing the bones he asked me to present some money for him. Maybe it was Korean custom, but I did not like it because everywhere I went, they were asking for money. Then when they presented me with the ashes, it was wrapped in white paper. The crematorium did not have a box to put the ashes and yet they took the money. I realized the dying needed more money than the living.

The bus returned us to my mom's home. When we arrived, everyone left me with my sister. My mother had left me instructions on what to do with her ashes, where to dispose of her body. Mother had told me while I was caring for her in July that if I was with her while she was dying to touch her body so that she could take any sickness from me. Her ashes were scattered at the 38th Parallel in the Im-Gin River so that she would be able to watch over me. She also requested that five days after her ashes were scattered in the Im-Gin River, a bunch of mums be thrown at the same spot. I knew why she requested specific details. My mother knew she had to visit her home, North Korea, before she left the Earth.

As I sat with my sister at the bus station, I asked her to come along with me. I liked to accompany her because I may not see her at all again. Since Mother was gone, there was no other way I could keep her. In truth, scattering the ashes by myself would be a scary experience but she refused to come with me. In fact, she never wanted to see me again because of how I was living my life and she hated my guts. She thought that I could have a job at the factory instead of working in the sauna and she went her own way. My bus arrived and I said good-bye to my sister and hopped on the bus. I began my journey to Im-Gin River. On the bus, I sat in the back because I did not want anyone to see my tears. I held my mother's crushed bones on a white paper. The ashes were still hot and it was heavy on my hands so I laid them on my lap throughout the whole trip. I thought that my mother was resting on my lap. It was a good feeling that I could be able to take care of her at last.

After the bus dropped me at my destination, I had to stop at the Korean Army checkpoint to show my ID and explain the reason for my trip. At the checkpoint, the soldiers called for an escort. In a few minutes, there were two soldiers coming to the gate and they took me into the compound where I could get a boat. My escort turned me over to someone who could row me out on the river where I could scatter the ashes. The way the soldier was looking at me was odd; I was young and there was no one with me. Besides, it was late afternoon and the sun was going down but I was planning on scattering the ashes. I could see the soldier's eyes were filled with curiosity if I had any other family members. I told him that if he had any question I had an answer. The soldier saw my tears were starting to fall and he became quiet and left me with my thoughts as he rowed me to the middle of the river. As I scattered the ashes, I prayed in silence that she would have an incredible journey going home.

It was getting darker and I needed to leave that place. I thanked him for his kindness and told him that I would be back in five days at my mom's request. He gave me his name and said to make sure I asked for him on my return. The soldier rowed me back and walked with me to the checkpoint. I felt relieved because at least I did all my work and Mother should be happy, I thought.

I was angry at both my mom and Sung Ha when I boarded the bus. As I sat in the back of the bus, I noticed my black outfit was covered with something that sparkled when the sun hit it. I realized it was Mother's ashes, which had blown on me when I scattered them, and my hands smelled of death, even though I was wearing gloves. My tears fell unbidden. In order to drown out my anger, I decided to go to the club where Sung Ha had worked. My whole plan was to get drunk and forget about what had happened. An hour after I arrived at the club, I found a table in the darkest corner so that no one recognized me. I ordered five large bottles of beer and started gulping them down fast as I could. I felt great because I hadn't had food in my stomach for who knew how long. When I was on the second bottle I felt a little dizziness, but I did not care. I was almost finishing the last bottle when the club owner came over to my table. He told me to stop drinking because I had had too much to drink. He said to me that he understood how I felt about losing my mom but I snapped at him. "What did you know about my mom, aha?"

Then I started to cry. He could have left me alone but he didn't; he knew about all the details of the story that shook all over town with Sung Ha. No one ever thought that I had such a vicious personality hidden under the surface but at that moment even he agreed how bad Sung Ha was. He continued talking a little more about Sung Ha. The night Sung Ha returned from the police station, he called him after midnight. Sung Ha came to the club and drank until he couldn't even walk so he took him to his home. Then he decided not to work there any more the very next day because of the embarrassment I had caused him. I told the club owner I couldn't care less. I was feeling no pain as I heard what he said about Sung Ha. The club owner told me to go home and rest, and tomorrow would be another day and I would start fresh. I thanked him. "At least, you understand how I feel," I'd said. I also told him that I'd just tossed my mother's ashes. As he walked away, I requested a dancer. I danced a couple of songs and sat down with a dancer drinking more beers. Several hours later I went home.

At work, no one bothered to say anything. They knew what had happened with my mom but everyone was afraid because they had experienced what kind of human being I was. The next five days passed in a blur, but I felt as if I had a millstone around my neck. My heart was in shreds and I had so many scars layered one over another. I did not know how to heal them and myself but I kept pushing on. On the morning of the fifth day, I bought a bouquet of white mums and a bottle of whiskey for the soldier as mother had requested that I must scattered flowers where her ashes had been spread. Before I left home, I dressed in a Korean folk dress. I got on the bus and it took me to the 38° parallel at the Korean Army checkpoint. I asked for the soldier who had helped me five days ago. At the gate, the soldier called for him but he couldn't come so instead he sent his friend. His friend asked me what I had done to his friend the prior day I was on the river. He told me that he had been haunted by me since the day he had helped me. I told his friend that it was probably what he saw in me: a solitary woman who mourned so wretchedly that it couldn't be erased from his mind. I asked him, "Can you imagine what that kind of look is like? Most people have their family, but I don't." He continued saying that his friend requested for a transfer to a different division and it could be in South Korea. When we arrived at the boat site, the other soldier was waiting in the boat. He was happy to see me so I smiled. Two men rowed the boat to the middle of the river where ashes had been tossed. I asked them to circle around the boat and as the boat was circling around, I tossed flowers around and I mourned again for my mom. Then I shared the whiskey with both of them. The weather was scorching hot again. Both of them were drunk and they wanted to cool off their bodies because they could not take me to the checkpoint. One of them suggested that they should jump into the water and they did. I watched them because even if I wanted to go into the water, I did not know how to swim. I was feeling good to be out on the open area on the water. I felt that some kind of blockage on my chest was opened and I could breathe easily. When the soldiers came into the boat, we chatted a bit and they rowed me back to the boat site. They offered to walk me to the gate. As we walked, I thanked them for their kindness, hospitality, and wished them great success in their lives, and said a final goodbye to them.

On the way home, I stopped at the club again. This time, I was hoping that I would see Sung Ha. I was still very upset with what had occurred between us. This time he was at the club. I sat at a table in the back again where it was dark and the mirror was behind me. As I lifted my glass, I saw Sung Ha coming toward me and he stood by my table. I could tell he was very angry and felt he wanted to hit me. He told me he would like to talk and asked me to come outside. Without hesitation, I followed outside. He led me into the alley where he grabbed my neck and dragged me into a corner of the building. Then he started punching me in the stomach. As I hunched over to hold my stomach he kicked me in the back continuously. He did not say a word and I did not try to defend myself either because I felt I deserved it. It was one of those unfortunate circumstances in my life and I realized that it was too late for things to go back to what they once were. I also understood that when I love someone, I shouldn't have the law interfere. I did not understand what true love was. My idea of love was more than physical attraction. Love has its depth, its height, and its boundary. I had given all that I was to the man I cared about but I felt guilty because I took revenge on him. He was taking his anger, frustration and his embarrassment out on me. As a result, I took his punishment until he busted his toe open and quit kicking me. Finally, his friends came out and saw what was happening. His friends yanked him away from me and said to him, "She is just a woman and she does not have the place that you to hit (meaning I was a very small woman, 110 pounds). You dumb..."

I was still kneeling down and holding my stomach. Physically, I was badly hurt, but he did not break my spirit. As far as I remembered, no one had broken my will. I knew the bruises would go away but mentally I would always remember what he did to me. Shortly after, one of his friends came to see how I was doing. He offered to take me home but I refused. The man was Myung Ja's boyfriend and I did not want to get into any more trouble then I already was, and besides, I mistrusted many of Sung Ha's friends. Finally, he said to me, "At least I will take you to the taxi." I told him that would be fine. I finally made my way home in pain, and alone again around midnight. When I was taking a bath, I heard someone knocking on my door. I opened the door and there was Sung Ha leaning on the wall with bag of something. He said how sorry he was and that he never intended to hurt me so much. Then he showed me his broken toe which I had already seen while we were in the alley. Maybe he did not notice it then because he was filled with anger He handed me a bag and said, "You will be in more pain in the morning. I want you to take this medication tonight and put some cream on your back and front." As he stepped toward the stairs he said, "I'm sorry.

I tried to talk to you but I already had a girlfriend living with me and I knew it was very wrong what I did to you. But if you need anything come over and talk to my girlfriend." That was good enough for me. Several days later, Sung Ha's girlfriend came to visit me. She knew all about what had happened. She apologized for Sung Ha's behavior and told me that if she had known about the need I had at the time, she could have avoided me going to the police station. She had a depth of personality and understood why I had made critical decisions about my mother. We became great buddies for the next year and a half. We shopped together and we went to travel to Pu San by the ocean where we made many good memories for a week. I never shared such a bond with anyone before her but she was the first woman that I did things with as an adult. Then eventually she also left Sung Ha because he started looking for another woman. She came to see me one more time and said she would be opening her own coffeeshop in downtown Seoul, that I should come to visit her. On that day, I saw her last smile on her face.

As I watched the bus drive way, my final thought crept into my mind. *This is how my first relationship ended.* I blamed my mother for everything because if she had not died I wouldn't have needed the money to take care of her funeral, and thus the incident with Sung Ha would never have happened. Somehow all my anger toward Sung Ha was in my heart melting like ice. He was a part of me even if I was moving on and he stayed with me for a very long time, even after I got married to an American G. I.

Eight

My mother had been gone for a year. I went to the Buddhist temple near Seoul and asked monks to pray for her. It was my duty as firstborn, and it was right thing for me to do just in case her spirit was still hovering around above my shoulders. I explained to the monks who my mother was, and how she lived her life. Unfortunately, she gave up her life, and eventually, I wanted to understand who my mother was. I did things for her out of my way even after her death so that her spirit might cross over accordingly. As I did each thing for her, my anger permeated so deeply and sadness hardened in my heart as years passed. My scars were plastering the walls of my heart and soon I could not talk about anything to anyone, but I had to move on for the future.

As I was leaving the temple, I thought about my mother once more and hoped that she would rest in her spirit. I had a lot of Mom's things, and I had to rent my home in Young Cho Gol in order to move all her things into my home. Her furniture, her clothes, etc... It seemed to me she was still alive and lived with me in my room and the thought gave me comfort. I felt that I had a place called home which I'd never had, and Mom was with me every step of my life. I quit working at the Turkish bath and found a job in Seoul. I was working as a maid in a hotel and the work was hard. Even though there wasn't much physical work, my health was poor. I was extremely exhausted, physically and mentally.

I experienced hallucinations. It was an early fall; I was so sick and couldn't get up so one of the ladies I worked with told me to go to rest and she would take care of the rest of my work. I found an empty room in an upstairs corner. As soon as my head hit the pillow I fell into a deep sleep. I dreamed my mom came to me and took hold of my right arm. I knew my mom was right there then. I was startled and ran to where my manager was. She thought there was something wrong with me because my body was soaked from sweat and my mouth was dry. My eyes were sunken. I explained what I saw in my dream and how Mom had touched me. I showed her my arm and there was an imprint of my mom's hand on my right arm. The manager explained to me that my mom knew I was really sick and losing consciousness so she tried helping me to get up.

Furthermore, her interpretation of my dream was that my mom cannot leave me because she promised to watch over me. For some reason, after mom's dream, I was able to function better in my daily life. When I went home for the weekends, I did manage to get the rest I needed. In particular, I felt safe, comfortable, and enjoyed my time off from work in my home. For the next few months, there wasn't much excitement in my life. It was the right time for me to rest my body, mind and spirit. I just took it easy on myself for the first time in my entire life.

The late fall of the same year I used a tailor across street from the hotel to make custom suits and a dress. I would wear that dress to clubs almost every night. I just wanted to get out of work and had fun in the clubs. Next door to the tailor shop, there was a classical music store. I never hear this kind of music before and it made my ear very happy. I was used to listening to old Korean folk music and I was falling in love with a totally different tune. On the street, I heard the music everyday; the music store played the records at 10 a.m. to midnight. The music store had two large speakers on the front of the store and it was nonstop playing the most beautiful music ever. One evening, I was ready to catch the bus when I heard music which made my heart sing and it moved me to go into the store to find out what it was. I had never been exposed to instrumental sound before and I wanted to have that piece right then. I stepped into the store, knowing that I'd be missing the bus. In the store, there was a young man at the counter. I asked him what that music was. He said, "It is the theme from Doctor Zhivago." He showed me an album but I couldn't buy it because I didn't have a record player. He said, "You can buy a small tape player," and he showed me a tape player. I purchased it and a tape. Instead of going out that night to the club, I went to my home. It was the most exciting moment in my life and that was the most powerful life experience ever, and I related to certain music from that point on. I found what I liked to enjoy most of my time when I was not working. I started purchasing four or five tapes a week: Beethoven's "Moonlight Sonata," Vivaldi's "Winter" (The four Seasons), Tchaikovsky "Swan Lake", and more. The rhythm transported me far away from this lonely place. The only friend I had was music, which I clung to like a life preserver. I still had emotional battles within, but when I was alone with music, I could forget for the moment.

I was constantly moving from job to job. I just couldn't seem to ground myself in any one place. Even though the music lifted my spirits for a short time, I was still trying to figure out what my future would be. I was sick of working at the hotels as a maid, at the Turkish baths, coffee shops, restaurants, and succumbing to other people's desires. I was ready to make changes in my life but did not know where to start. I had no education, no job skills, no one to give me direction. In my empty room, I thought about my options many days and nights, and then all of suddenly a thought arrived from somewhere.

I did remember while I was working at the Turkish bath that there were many American servicemen I had encountered. I realized how different those men were from the Korean men. Americans were more considerate of women and they did not treat me like a slave, as Korean men did. I did not know the language but I knew what they wanted from me. I liked these yellow haired men very much. They were naïve, humble, and gentle men like lambs whom I could easily lead. I felt that American men respected me for the kind of job I had. I also loved to eat peanut butter, jelly and toast which I was able to purchase on the black market. Many different places I worked, the owners told me that I should marry a "Yankee" (This is an expression for all Americans in Korean). I made my final decision to change my job to where the Americans were. It was a critical decision because there would be no turning back when I got into an American club. In the spring of 1984, I talked to a club owner in Young Chu Gol. The owner owned the American club and the club would be moving to a different place where American soldiers came to train in Korea. It was called The Team Spirit 1984; this was where the American troops would come and stay in training for four to six months in the field. I decided to follow them and experience a different lifestyle. I did not speak English but someone would translate for me.

The club was set up temporarily for next four to six months, and I finally arrived. I stepped into the club, and the club was filled with smoke, smelling of stale beers and had dim lights. I remembered that I used to like sitting quietly in a dark corner somewhere like this place before. The first night, the first man walked up and asked me to dance. I did not know how to dance but I watched a couple of people in the club. The man introduced himself to me as Paul and he was from New York. He asked me what my name was, but I did not understand so I called a co-worker and she came and talked to Paul for a moment. She told me that my name would be Miss Choe. Paul and I danced one song and he asked me to sit at the table. He walked away for a few minutes and I thought that he had left. When he returned to me he had a long stemmed rose in his mouth and his teeth were holding the rose. As he sat down on the chair, he handed the rose to me and asked me if I was available. At this point, I had to call someone again to interpret what he was saying. After the interpreter left, Paul and I left the club together. I couldn't see clearly what he was looked like because it was so dark but in the light, he was good looking. He had blond curly hair, buck teeth with a cute freckled face, and was about 5'5". He was gentle and stroked my whole body like he was touching beautiful flowers. We spent the night in the motel and he had to leave early in the morning and he kissed me goodnight. When I woke up, he already left and I thought it was just one night. The next evening, Paul showed up at the club and brought me another long stem rose and asked me to dance with him. I began to like this man very much and each night, I would sit in the same corner hoping that he would show up again.

I did not want to be with anyone else. Some nights I would turn away other men because I wanted to wait for Paul. In fact, if he did not stop by I felt sad, and when this happened, many men approached me to find out what was making me sad. Since I still did not speak English, it made it difficult to explain and I'd rather not said anything to anyone. Although, I was very curious as to why they even cared about me. I was comparing either side of the cultures; Korean men never asked, but with American men if they saw I was not smiling, they came over to my table and asked me, "What's wrong?" I usually just shrugged my shoulders and shook my head. They usually stayed with me and bought a drink for me. I had given up liquor so I would drink orange juice. I did not know Americans could be such respectful, gentle, and caring people. I was used to the disrespect shown by most Korean men. Perhaps it was the way American men were raised by his or her parents and taught by the Army. During this time, I met less aggressive people and also many American soldiers who were very generous to me financially. Although, this was a confusing time for me, it also filled my life with endless excitement.

The Team Spirit tour was coming to an end, and I had to make the crucial choice of my life. I had to choose which road to take— whether I was going to stay in the American club or go back to a Korean club. My choice was obvious because I tasted what it was like to be with Americans and my decision was to stay with Americans, and I moved near the Air Force Base in Osan, Southeast from Seoul. Most of all Air Force clubs were very large, and I had never seen one before. For the first time, I noticed segregation between blacks and whites. The Korean club owner seemed to know which girls would fit with either the blacks or the whites, and I was placed in the white club and started work. The day went by quickly because I did not feel I was working. More or less, I was having fun. I had a short trip to Team Spirit and I was in a different environment, an environment where there were live beats and the soldiers were happy and light-hearted when they were drunk. I did not have to drink but at the same time I enjoyed just being there with the flow of the music.

Like any other club owner, this club owner also noticed that I was different from all the other girls that had passed through. The club owner was interested in my life story and when we had a chance, we talked about my life story. After what she heard about me she gave me advice. She said that I should marry the first American solider who asked me to marry him. She further explained that she had seen so many tragic things happen to the girls who stayed in the club for long periods of time. She didn't want me to end up like the other girls; she could not forget the memories of them. She also said that I just stepped into the club and chances of finding a man to marry would be numerous because most men were looking for women treating them like being something supreme.

This was the first time I received inspiration from a Korean woman and she touched me deep in my heart. She actually treated me like a human being. This woman saw beyond the club girl and realized I had a loving spirit and the potential to be something better. She went on to explain me that many Korean women who married Americans got divorced and end up back in Korea working at the clubs again. When these women stepped into the club, their chance of remarrying was slim to none. She believed that I would be fine because she recognized that I had my inner strength, and I also had incredible thought processing skills. I would survive even being in another country, and I would make it to the end of my life. She must have recognized part of herself in me. Then she went on saying that life's offerings were not easy to obtain. If I wanted to obtain greatness in life, there were many hills to climb, and a lot of difficulties to face all alone. I already faced many difficulties all alone, so it should be a little easier. She said she pursued her goals even when she got discouraged, and every step she took forward made her life better and better and life got a little easier.

I had been working this club for several months, and I met a decent man who helped me financially. Unfortunately, I became very ill and I had to quit the club. My illness was unknown. The symptom of my illness was that I would swell up from the waist down and it was difficult to sit or walk. Therefore, I did clean at the club occasionally and my debts were getting higher every day. One day when I was cleaning the club as usual, a sergeant walked in. His name was David, his rank was E-6 and he was working at the D.M.Z. 38° parallel in Korea, near where I had spread Mother's ashes.

Every so often I heard the rumors about him through the other girls in the club. The girls told me that he was strange because he never talked or smiled and he was always alone. However, when he started talking to me, I thought he was a good man. David was unusually quiet and always spoke softly. He was very thin like my dad, but blond, about 6'2". He had blue eyes that were sunken behind glasses with black frames. He was like the person most people thought "creepy." He also had scars on his cheeks and his hands. He was not very attractive but I was a caring person; I took this man under my wings. Every night he would come to the club and pay for drinks but he never drank. He took me out so I wouldn't have to work. Eventually, he asked me to move in with him and we spent the winter together in my rented house. We had a very tight budget because the money he brought to me monthly was very little, and yet, it was better than what I was earning. So, I took in laundry from the neighbors. In order to make money despite the how cold winter weather, I had to wash all the laundry by hand and use a washboard outside on the courtyard. Each month, with his small paycheck and what I made from laundry, we managed to scrape by, and the grocery store owner gave me credit once in a while. It was alright because I felt that I was getting better and I had less worries about where I would be tomorrow.

We had been living together for a couple of months and David proposed to me. He said that he would send me a fiancée visa when he returned to the United States. He also told me that it's better to send all my things before he left Korea. I agreed and packed up most of all my things and shipped them to his mother in Philadelphia. The things I packed were family pictures, Korean dresses which I had made for my mother before she died, and other incidental things that I do not remember now. David was busy preparing to depart and each time he left home, he took all my boxes to ship them to the United States. All my belongings had been shipped to the United States, and one night I had a strange dream. *In the dream, there was a boiler technician, whom I used to know in Seoul. He came to escort me in my dream and asked me to follow him. I followed him to the dock. At the dock, there was a cruise ship that had docked, and the body of the ship was painted in rainbow colors on her body. Her body had seven lines of rainbow colors freshly painted. The ship was ready to depart the harbor, and we got into the ship just in time. The technician led me to a boiler room where he threw a switch and the sound like the huge generator was running really fast. As the generator's belt was turning faster, in the middle of the boiler room, there was rice falling from the ceiling on one side, and sea salt falling from the ceiling on other side of the belt. As the pile of sea salt became higher, I discovered something else in the piles of salt. I asked the technician to shut off the motors. I plowed through deeper in the salt with my hands, and I retrieved my mother's body.*

I picked her up and carried her out of the ship, and laid her on my bed. When I woke up, I was drenched through my clothes with sweat and my face had been streaked by tears. I thought it was strange and it bothered me for a while. I did not know what else to make of this dream because I would soon be moving away from Korea but I did not think of as it was a warning. David returned home about two weeks after the dream but I did not tell him anything. I did not want to cause any problems in our relationship.

Near the end of January 1984, David went to work as usual. The weather was severely dropping in temperature, and we were going to get a lot of snow. I was washing laundry outside as usual and I felt pretty good that morning. By afternoon, the club owner was at my door, out of her breath. She told me that David had a wife who showed up at the club. His wife was upset and was looking for her husband and me. His wife showed her a picture of David and me together. That picture was taken by a professional photographer for our anniversary. I had no idea he was married. The club owner described his wife as a heavyset Korean woman who had no class whatsoever. She was loud and disrupted the club as she stepped into the door. She had her two beautiful daughters with her and they had been living only 50 miles from where we lived. David had been lying to both of us, and in this situation, I didn't know what to think. Instead of going to work every day, he must have been going to see his family. My head was spinning and my heart was broken. I was standing in the blizzard cold but could not feel anything. *Why do bizarre things happen to me? Why am I so unlucky?* I was feeling sorry for myself and I wanted to know why was I beaten down by so many people emotionally. In my head there were many questions forming without answers.

After the club owner left, David's wife came to see me. She behaved atrociously but I let her in the room. Her size and her anger filled the room. She accused me of being a home wrecker. I tried to explain that I didn't know David had a family but she did not hear any of my words. In my head there was a sound of her voice echoing a thousand miles away and I could hear her last words. "Send my husband back home." She left the room. My tears rolled down, and I cried soundlessly for a long time. I felt that something inside of me was saying that I better get a grip on myself before David got home. He had the nerve to return that night. Maybe he did not know his wife had dropped by our house that day. I was angry but I did not show my feelings to him, and I told him that I wanted to fetch my friend who spoke English well because I had to talk to him about something important.

I went to the club and asked a friend who could speak English, and she came to my home to be my translator. The translator told David what had happened. He became pale and he said to me sorry because he lied about being married. It was very painful for me to tell someone who had helped me the way he did, but I had to tell him to return to his wife and children. I also told him to try to make his marriage work and be happy. He quietly listened to what I said to the translator and he cried. He told me the truth about his unfortunate childhood and his horrible marriage, and he continued saying that he was afraid to return to his wife and children. He tried to tell the truth to me many times but he did not have the courage to tell me about his situation. I pushed him out anyway that night. It was still dropping in temperature but I knew he could get to his family. He was gone for good and I suddenly realized many dear things were now lost to me because they had been shipped to the United States.

Since David left, the weather got little warmer, and I did not feel so lost anymore. David had been gone for a week or two and I thought he was in the United States. One day I opened the door to find David standing there. He had come back to see me and said that he had filed for a divorce. He said this was what he and his wife had wanted for a long time. He asked me if he could stay with me until his divorce was final. I took him back because he had nowhere else to go. He also said to me if I was with him when he meets his ex-wife I would give him tremendous courage; it may have been true because every time he had to meet with his wife and her lawyer, she was in a combative mood and I was beside David at all times.

In the spring of 1984, David's divorce was finalized and he had to leave Korea. I packed everything for him and we had a tearful goodbye. He still told me he would send me a fiancé visa when he got to the United States. I'd thought he had left Korean soil, however, my neighbor's husband Cleaby (who worked at Camp Howze), brought me news I had never expected. According to Cleaby, apparently the military police caught up with David at the airport. David was AWOL. Cleaby said that David wanted to see me in the jail. Next morning, Cleaby and I took the first bus running to the jail where David was being held. According to Cleaby, David would be taken away after he saw me, and the Military Police would escort him to the United States. He would be serving his time there. It was a beautiful spring morning when I talked to David and I thanked him for sticking by me during my illness. Truly, this was the last time I would see him ever because I did not know where the United States was.

Cleaby and I took the bus home and Cleaby hugged me. I knew that he felt really sorry for me going home alone and who knew when I would be meeting another man? Yet, I felt relieved and found freedom. Perhaps I did not realize how hurt I had been. I had built a wall around myself so that no one could break through. I knew I needed to keep moving forward, whether I realized it or not. This experience was slowly but surely another turning point in my life.

Nine

Shortly after David left, I had to return to work. The season changed to early summer and I was hired by another club, a few buildings down from the street where I met David. This club also catered to American servicemen. A few months passed and I was just getting by. I took one day at a time but still had debts to pay. It was late afternoon July 21, 1984. The longest monsoon season just ended. I had to open the club that day a little earlier than usual because the weather was cloudy and chilly. I had to change the charcoal, set up the room, and stock the bar in the kitchen. In the late afternoon, suddenly as the door was opening two servicemen walked in. These men had loud voices and they walked in like they won some kind of prize. One of the men I knew previously because he was customer of my friend. The other serviceman was a new face. My friend's customer came up to the counter, pointed at the new face and said, "This is Turtle," (which was an expression for new people arriving at the Army Base) and they sat on a table near the counter. They kidded around with me and asked where Sue was. I called the club owner to send Sue to the club. Shortly, she came into the club and introduced Turtle.

My first impression of Turtle, (whose real name was Thomas) was that he was tall and skinny, but good-looking. His head was shaved like a monk in Korea, and he had beautiful hazel eyes. He looked like an arrogant officer who had much pride in himself. They were both dressed in civilian clothes. Thomas was wearing gray shorts with a burgundy Army T-shirt. I quickly read this new man as I took their orders, and Sue was sitting by both of them but she was busy with another man. I noticed Thomas had a perplexed look on his face. I thought, for Thomas, everything must have been new to him since it was his first time in a foreign country. On the other hand, his friend must have been introducing him to Korean club life.

I had a wild imagination about this newcomer in my head and I heard Sue ask me to come to sit with them. I was introduced and sat with them but I didn't feel confident after meeting Thomas, but something inside told me that I was attracted to him. He had ordered a bottle of Heineken and I got a glass of orange juice. While I was sitting next to Thomas, I thought if he liked me, I might make some money. I still spoke broken English and could barely understand their conversation. I tried to be friendly and show some interest in their homeland. I was mainly interested in making money from them, but still felt an attraction toward Thomas. He didn't pay much attention to me while we were sitting at the table. I felt he was ignoring me but also I noticed that he kept looking at Sue. I swallowed my pride and pretended I didn't notice. I asked him when he had arrived in Korea. If I remember correctly, he landed on his twenty-first birthday, July 7, 1984. He was in basic training in the United States and shipped out to the D.M.Z. to the American Army Base. Here I was again: someone from the 38° parallel, D.M.Z., soon as I'd forgotten some thoughts of my mother. Thomas bought me another drink but I didn't feel welcome so I walked away and left the drink. As I walked away, I heard them giggling and was sure it was at my expense. They were spending time for awhile and I had another customer to take care of.

Sue was engaged to an American officer who was in the United States. Sue was working at the club until her fiancé could come back with a visa for her. Thomas spent a lot of time with her because she was sexy and had dyed her hair blonde like an American woman.

103

She was small featured and attracted every serviceman who came into the club. Sue's fiancé made arrangements for Sue to move out of the club and into a home he had secured for them. Thomas helped her move. Just before the move, Sue introduced Thomas to me again and it was the second time we met. This time he did not act superior. I guess that he had learned how to be polite or that day I may have seen his true being. The day was raining cats and dogs in a warm summer, in August or early September. Sue was doing his hair and soon as the rain stopped, she would be moving. Sue then asked me to give Thomas a back massage and she told him how good I was at giving a massage. Sue told Thomas that since she wouldn't be available because of her marriage, he should see me anytime he had an overnight pass. He promised me that he would come back to see me sometime.

A couple of months had been passed before I saw Thomas again. The weather was getting colder. It was very close to my birthday in November when Thomas returned from field training in the D. M. Z. He came to see me at the club. He was wearing black sweatpants with burgundy a sweatshirt. His winter jacket was a blended color of gray and black, and he had a knit cap. He walked right up to me and said, "I promised you I would come back." I was stunned. I never thought that he would really come to see me and I did not feel as uncomfortable as before. We talked easily but did not have much to say. We sat at the counter and had a drink or so and he told me that he had to leave. As he got up he assured me of the exact day he would return.

The day of his return happened to be my birthday but he was not aware of it. This was the fourth time we'd met, and I told Thomas that it was my birthday even though I celebrated it as a lunar birthday (* Lunar birthday meant the Chinese calendar, which most Koreans would consider the real day of birth). Truthfully, my birthday would be still one month away but Americans do not understand so I changed my birthday to the regular calendar date of November 13. Besides, he might have never have come to see me again. We had a couple of drinks and he asked me to go to the market down the street. He took me to the store and he bought me a pink ceramic piggy bank. I thanked him for my birthday present and we went to my room. He lay on my bed with his clothes on. I asked him a strange question. I had never asked anyone this before. The question was rather odd and it came out of nowhere. My question was to him was, "If a woman could not have a baby what would you do?" At that point I could still have children but the question to Thomas just came out. Thomas' answer was he would adopt a baby if a woman could not have his child. Somehow his answer was comforting to me at that moment without knowing why. That night, we had a short evening together the first time, and I did not know what was waiting in my future. From that night on, he came to see me on a regular basis, and sometimes he did not have an overnight pass but he always managed to come to see me. He was trustworthy and there were no other girls for him. While he was devoted to me, I had to work and keep earning money because I had bills to pay.

While I was seeing Thomas, I was also involved with an officer, who was Thomas' boss. I'd met him long before I met Thomas. Thomas' boss was compassionate, funny and always treated me like his girlfriend. He was married once, divorced and remarried. He showed me his second wife's picture and said that if he wasn't married, he would marry me. I thanked him and I told him I would too, because his friend was marrying a Korean girl. We both knew it was an impossible risk in our lives. When he returned to the United States, his current wife found our picture together in his pocket, and she asked him if he was coming back to her. He said to her he would be back, alone. Thomas' boss heard that I was seriously involved with Thomas and he wished and hoped that I would be happy with Thomas. He reminded me that Thomas was young and immature. It was an officer's friendly advice one last time. Thomas got promoted to E-8, and he was standing in the recreation room by the window.

He was wearing a white uniform with a white, gold trim hat, and he sent me a huge smile.

Thomas and I had known each other little over two months and it was Thanksgiving. He asked me to accompany him to the mess hall for Thanksgiving dinner. It was the first time someone asked me to be a date. I was filled with excitement because I had never seen a mess hall. I dressed in a green knit, long skirt which matched with Thomas' green uniform. When he came down to escort me into the base, I felt that I was different. At the mess hall table, we all saluted the United States flag and brief Thanksgiving prayers were read. I had never seen Thanksgiving dinner. It was delicious with a different taste. We enjoyed a wonderful and amazing Thanksgiving dinner together. Indeed, I was enjoying the American lifestyle, and I was envious of how these people lived.

I thought that I would like to learn all about American customs. Furthermore, I began comparing Korean customs to American customs and soon, I did not feel I was Korean anymore. I could not fit in with Korean customs any longer. After the dinner, Thomas introduced me to his buddies in his platoon. Thomas' platoon knew that he was crazy about me and I felt the same about him. I still didn't speak English well so Thomas wrote down what I should say when I called for him in the barracks. At least, I knew how to read English so Thomas wrote on a piece of paper, "May I speak to (his rank) Thomas, please." I memorized this one sentence for a very long time and each time someone said something I wrote on a piece of paper, and it was the only way I could learn to speak.

About a week had past after Thanksgiving. Thomas asked me if we could live together. I said yes to him without hesitation because I remembered the old woman who gave me advice to marry the first man who asked me, and in fact, I was really ready to give up the club life and settle down with one man. I told Thomas honestly that I owed money to the club owner. He called his mom and asked her to send money. I did not know how he asked her to send money and for what reason. The amount I requested from Thomas was the money he got from the G.I. Bill, and I found this out many months later.

When the check had arrived, Thomas came to the club. It was enough money to pay off my debt, rent a house, and to buy household goods and furniture. I was dreaming about having my own place and being with Thomas. I had hope. Thomas promised me he would pay the club owner off so I would be free. I wasn't sure it was real because I was living my life without trusting anyone; therefore, I did not know what real love was. I thought that I did love Thomas. He was seven years younger than me but he cared about me very much and he had compassion for me. However, I was still cautious about our relationship because many people had hurt me previously. Also, people around me constantly told me that people lie whether they aware of it or not. I still had reservations about trusting Thomas completely. After all, he was a serviceman, and if he was shipped out where he would leave me? He hadn't paid my debt yet and until he did, I still had to work. However, once he paid the debt, for the first time in my life I was amazingly happy. I just wanted to hold him forever and keep him happy as long as I lived.

We found a nice house closer to Camp Howze. We had one bedroom, a kitchen, and an outhouse. Although we did not have a shower, it wasn't a big deal because Thomas could use the Army base facility and I went to the Korean bathhouse. The house owner and his family were super nice people and always included us for meals together. Sometimes, they gave us supplies and helped me in many ways so we quickly became good friends. At the same time, Thomas still had to bunk on base so I was alone at night until he could get a weekend pass or overnight pass to stay with me. Since I couldn't work or I didn't go anywhere during the day, my friendship with the landlord and his family meant a lot to me. This family also trusted Thomas because one of the family members who worked at Camp Howze knew Thomas very well. I was glad to hear that Thomas was a good man and that comforted me. Whatever happened I thought I was going to be alright.

In mid-December of 1984, Thomas came home. He stood in the kitchen and leaned on the bedroom door. I thought something was wrong because I did not know what else to ask, besides, I could not speak English. Before he took his boots off, he knelt down by the bedroom door and asked, "Will you marry me?" I was stunned. I thought, *Getting me out of the club wasn't enough, now he wants me to be his wife? What a wonderful word can a woman expect to hear from a man? Am I going to get married?* They were incredible thoughts and feelings that showered over me and I could not breathe. At that moment in my life Thomas was the most wonderful person I ever met, and my hero. There was nothing in the world I could or would worry about. He pulled me out of hell on earth, and gave me freedom from all my sufferings. That was what I felt. We still had language barriers, but that didn't matter because we needed each other so I accepted his marriage proposal. "Yes, I will marry you," I'd said. It was an awesome Christmas present I never had before.

We started the necessary steps for the paperwork in order to get married. The first step was to hire a Korean professional who had been assisting numerous Korean women marrying American serviceman. The second step was to resister all the paperwork with the Korean City Hall and the American Embassy. The third step was to be interviewed at the American Embassy about the description of my job, what I was doing when I met Thomas, whether I knew Thomas' family by letters, pictures and how often I spoken to them. I had to know Thomas' family names, histories etc. Thomas' family had sent me all necessary information that I needed for the interviews. Especially, his mom was 100% behind us from the beginning to the end. The interview was more of an interrogation than an interview but I didn't feel nervous.

Apparently, we both passed the interviews because our paperwork was processed favorably. The next step was to find the Chaplin at the Camp Howze church to set up counseling sessions.

At the end of the last session, the Chaplin told us to have fun in the bedroom, and keep each others' life happy. I was officially married now, and I had free access to the base, commissary, and laundry facilities. Above all, I could go to see medical doctors, dentists, and ENT doctors. Indeed, within a few months, I was becoming used to changes in my daily chores, and I was attending English classes on base or went off the base freely. At the same time, I found a Korean private school that taught English by a Korean teacher. My instructor was born in the United States, lived in Hawaii, and had gotten married to a Korean woman and had a child. He decided to move to Korea to teach English as Second Language, but also, he wanted his child to know about father's origin. He was my instructor who was impressed with the way I pronounced English words and told me that I would have no problems in the United States. I was non-stop going to English classes. As one class ended, I signed up for more. I had an unquenchable thirst for learning, and that was the time I had to push harder and harder to fulfill what I needed the most. In this way, at least, I understood when Thomas spoke to me.

We finally got officially married April 17, 1985. The marriage document was stamped by the American Embassy and the Korean Seoul City Hall. Even though we were officially married on a piece of paper as husband and wife, I told Thomas that I would rather have a wedding ceremony in the United States. In truth, I didn't have my family or any close friends for me but Thomas did. Thomas agreed and understood. In addition, I would rather have Thomas' father walk me down the aisle. I devoted my life to my husband and his family even if we were 3,000 miles away. I missed his family and began to understand how comforting Thomas was walking with me the rest of my life. During this time, Thomas was also busy getting my Social Security card from California while we were in Korea. Strangely, all the steps of marriage paperwork went through smoothly and it took us three and half months. It was unusual because the entire marriage process finally ended in three-and-a-half months.

Kateleen K. Washington

In the summer of 1985, Thomas had to make a critical decision about whether he could stay one more year or go back to the United States. I asked him to stay one more year in Korea for two reasons. The first reason was I wanted to learn more English and I needed more time to prepare for coming to the United States (however, I wanted to move away as soon as I could). The second reason was we had to save some money before we left Korea. Thomas understood. For these reasons, he requested one more year of duty in Korea. As soon as the Army accepted Thomas' reenlistment, we took a two-week vacation for our honeymoon. I had seen one part of South Korea and I wanted to see the other half; this was a great opportunity for us to explore.

I scheduled the plan because we had a budget, so we could spend less money on the road. My plan was to travel by train and bus. The first day, we took the night train from Seoul to Pu San, and by doing so, we saved time and money by sleeping on the train. We arrived at about sunrise, where we could see the South Coast in the morning. We walked along the beach. At the end of the beach, we took our pictures on the rocks. It was the most beautiful I had ever seen because this time visiting with my husband made me feel much more sentimental and I would remember forever. We then arrived at the bus station, and had breakfast. I purchased two bus tickets to Kyong Chu where most of the Korean dynasty history was kept in one place. In the bus, at the checkpoint, Korean Military Police came up to the bus and asked us for ID. Thomas showed his ID and I showed mine. As much as I hated Korean men, I kept my mouth shut even if those men said something I did not want to hear.

Along the bus ride, we saw many neat places and finally we arrived to see the Korean dynasty histories. There, we saw the biggest and tallest Buddha statues, and visited the most famous Buddha Temples in Korea. From there, we caught the bus again and went north up the Coast of East Sea. We finally went through the mountains of East Coast, across rivers, and we were on 99 winding hills of the freeway (later reminding me of the Ozark Mountains). Several hours of bus ride later, we arrived at the Sul Ak Mountain National Park. Mt. Sul Ak, the highest mountain in Korea located at the far Northeast, is closer to North Korea. I could say it was the place of Heaven on Earth. There were miles and miles of Asian pine groves and all this natural scenery, landscape, rare plants, and trees I had never seen before. When we looked up, we could not see the summit of the mountains clearly, covered by the mystic clouds. It took us several hours to walk to the mountain road and we came to the top of the mountain. We encountered a forest ranger who looked more like a wild mountain man and he knew every detail of the mountains. He was interested in our visit and he explained to us the different way of life on the mountain. He told us that he could not live in the modern city. I believed him.

We took our time and stayed one or two nights at each stop. Everywhere we went people were generous and really good to us because these people hadn't seen an American. Our next stop was below the ocean level, under the tunnel. In the tunnel, stone had been forming, growing thousands of years and it attracts many tourists. The rock formations were a spectacle and we were amazed by their unusual beauty. It was the most wonderful and romantic honeymoon in Korea and we made a lasting impression in our memories. We weren't in a hurry and wanted to enjoy the scenery and each other's company. Thomas was amazed at the beauty of Korea and I became frisky.

Sometimes, we stayed in a hotel; the food was excellent, tasty; even though they used the same kind of spices but it had a different taste. The hotel was located in the deep forest, and when we got up to open the window, we smelled the nature.

I relied on Thomas very much emotionally and nothing bothered me anymore. It was only one week of our honeymoon but one spent in heaven, I'd thought. I knew his trip was my first and it would be the last because I would never want to step on Korean

111

soil again. This trip was my goodbye to my past but Thomas had no idea. On the other hand, Thomas learned there was much more to Korea than what he had seen in the club. When we returned from our journey, Thomas told everyone in his platoon how wonderful the trip was. From there on, when Thomas had leave, he wanted to go different places in Korea see more history about Korea. Besides our honeymoon, we visited several places in Korea and he respected and remembered it.

The honeymoon was over and we were back to reality. He went to work and I attended school for English as a Second Language program, at the 8th Army Division in Seoul Young San. Each day, I rode a bus from Camp Howze in Pong IL Chen to Young San Seoul, which was an hour one-way. Most days, I was in class when Thomas wasn't home because he had field training. One day I was in the class, my instructor told me to go outside and there would be someone waiting for me by the picnic table. My heart was beating fast because no one I knew would have found me there. With excitement and curiosity, I went out and there was Thomas standing by the picnic table with a big grin on his face. He brought my lunch and it was rice and kimchi (it is made of cabbages or turnip marinated in sea salt and hot seasoning). I was surprised by his incredible gesture. He couldn't speak Korean but managed to take a civilian bus from Camp Howze to Young San. He could have taken the military bus, but the bus schedule from the Camp Howze to Young San wasn't available so he had to take a Korean bus. It was near my lunchtime and he did not want to miss it. When he got on the bus and told the bus driver where he was going, he had correctly given him the bus fair with Korean currency.

I was overwhelmed by his thought and deep heart; he cared about me in a way I never expected. Without knowing Korean culture or language he was a courageous man, and he was a sweet man. I knew I would be fine living with him the rest of my life. Through his voluntary action, I realized that he did love me and he cared about me. He was the first person in the whole world who did not know who I was, and it did not matter to him at all. While we were in Korea, we did not need to speak and we knew each other from our hearts. While I was talking to him I forgot about my lunch and Thomas reminded I should eat my lunch. Suddenly, I found that I had a voracious appetite. Thomas was smiling while I stuffed down my lunch and he'd said, "Slow down, you will get sick." I was happy.

Things were moving slowly and positively in both school and marriage. Then one day in the beginning of the fall we got a puppy. It was a small, long fluffy haired and multicolored mutt. To me, it looked like a small bear so we named it Gomdoli ("bear" in English). We loved that puppy. We used to play, and it slept with us all the time, even though Korean culture wouldn't allow it. In the winter of 1985, Thomas and I took Gomdoli out to the temple where kings and queens' headstones lay nearby. The day was overcast and began to snow but we did not notice. We were having such a great time playing hide and seek with our puppy. Two of us took some pictures and about six months later, the puppy disappeared from our lives. We did not know what happened to him. I still cannot remember how I lost my dog.

In the spring of 1986, I called Mrs. Park again because I wanted to let her know that I was married, and I would be leaving Korea in the near future. Mrs. Park was shocked by absolutely incredible news that she ever heard from me. She was very happy and welcomed me as if her own daughter had been married. She wanted to see both of us in her home and she would make reservations in a restaurant. I made the schedule to see her with Thomas when he was off. I was relieved because the last time I saw her was four years ago, before my mother passed away. I hung up the phone with her and the same night, when Thomas returned from work, I told him that we had to go to see Mrs. Park. Thomas was excited by the news. He thought I had no one. I did not like to think about my past.

About a week later, we went to see Mrs. Park. I always considered Mrs. Park the closest person to my mother, so she was my mother. I told Thomas to wear his gray suit. I wanted my husband to be a good and well mannered American who respected Korean culture. I was wearing a formal dress when we visited her. Mrs. Park kindly greeted us as if we were her family. She spoke fluent English and Thomas was impressed by his surroundings. He was comfortable carrying conversations with her and on the other hand, I did not know what they were sharing. She looked still the same even though she'd lost her husband. We shared coffee and afterwards, she took us to a marvelous restaurant at the Hyatt in Seoul Young San which was at the top of a mountain. In the restaurant, she was like a real mother and at that moment, all my past difficulties disappeared. Thomas and Mrs. Park talked most of the time and I would pay attention to their conversation actively. I understood what they were saying about me. After lunch, we returned to her home and she told me she would love to give me a wedding gift. It would be a custom-made wedding dress. We thanked Mrs. Park and went home. Thomas was impressed, saying she was a classy person with money but overall, she was a good person.

I had to go to Seoul several times for the dress fitting, and when it was completed, I had the most beautiful gift I ever received from anyone. My dress was white with a fitted bodice, and with ruffled quarter-length sleeves. It had a long skirt under which I had to wear a hooped slip to keep the skirt flared. The entire dress was beaded with white pearls. The veil was attached to a pearl headband and it was about eight feet long. The dress also came with a clustered a set of pearl earrings, and also included a set of white gloves about three quarters length and it was made of the same material as the dress. Mrs. Park was there to see the final fitting. When I came out of the fitting room with the dress on, I was astonished by my look and left her speechless. She finally could speak and told me how gorgeous I looked in that dress. She took me to the shoe store and bought white heels to match the dress. It was about lunchtime and we ate pizza, which I had never tasted before. We chatted a little more in the Pizza Hut. She said that I had made the right choice; granted that I had lived awful life, and yet, I had lived honestly all those harsh years without complaint. And in return, eventually every sacrifice pays off in the end. She also told me that I had a long way to travel, so be strong, firm, determined and live my life undauntedly. Once more, I promised her that I would live best way possible with all my strength and thanked her for everything she had done for me. I hoped someday I would see her again in the United States. It was the one last insightful moment we had ever shared.

My life was on the fast track and seemed promising. There was nothing going wrong and I had confidence and strength as well as a sense of freedom. Then one night I had a dream that would haunt me for a very long time. I dreamed I was sitting on a metal chair in the middle of an empty interrogation room alone, and with a single light over my head. Then the dream changed its location. The place was then Camp Howze on the barricaded side of the wall. The wall was built around the way up the hillside. As I looked up along the wall my mom was coming down the hillside of Camp Howze. She was wearing a white Korean dress. The spotlight from the Camp was not very bright when I found her. She looked to be in agony and her expression was motionless. It seemed to me that something was wrong. Suddenly I woke up from this dream and cried. I didn't know why I was crying. There was no reason to be crying. I did not miss my mother, plus I did not want to remember what she had put me through as a child. I only thought about this dream briefly then pushed it to the back of my mind and went on with my life. However, this may have been the beginning of warnings to me about my future. My dreams about my mother would continue but I was not concerned about it because Thomas was there to protect me. I felt safe and no matter what kind of problem might arise, I would be fine as long as he was with me. Thomas, my husband, was my super hero, a protector, and I put him on a pedestal.

Thomas was gone field training twice a month. When he would return, he would bring his dirty, smelly, and rotten laundry in a duffle bag. No matter how many piles of dirty laundry he brought home, I washed it by hand with a washboard. When the Army uniform went into the water, it stiffened, and yet, I did not mind washing it. While I was washing, he would catch up on his lost sleep. He told me that when he was in the field training, he would not sleep or get very little sleep. When he woke up, he helped me carry the wet laundry hamper to the Laundromat in Camp Howze to use the dryer. When they dried, I would fold the clothes a certain way. I'd tried to teach Thomas how to fold correctly but he never got the hang of it. After we came home from the Laundromat, I had to iron all his uniforms using starch. It took me hours to finish ironing and in the meantime, Thomas would watch me iron or he watched television.

I did not realize that Thomas may have wanted to have sex often but he never made his intension clear to me. I thought a good wife's duties were to cook, to clean, to iron, etc. I never thought that sex was the most important part of marriage. My priority was to keep my husband happy and I had sex with him when he approached. My culture taught me that a woman should not say no to a husband whenever he approached, and most of the time I just did it because all I could think about was that if I lost him I would have no chance of surviving.

Ten

Nothing else in my life mattered to me, except keeping Thomas happy and my education. While Thomas was in field training, I would look for work but I could not find anything unless I returned to the club which I did not want to do. Therefore, I was overly frustrated often. However, I tried to find the way to relieve my frustration. I did not know this was a form of depression and when this happened I went to see Thomas. During the summer, he went to training at the D.M.Z. I missed him very much and during his absence, I wished I was a bird so that I could fly to him day and night and be right by beside him all the time. I was miserably bored. My husband was the only friend I could count on and I did not know how to express my feeling of being alone. I understood he had no choice, and I had to accept the way we were. Hence, I did not have a true close human relationship with anyone else; I began to feel isolated and I hid for a long time.

I met Thomas at the D. M. Z. outside of his tent. He looked exhausted by the summer heat. He told me he would be returning home briefly within a couple of days. I kissed him and hopped on the bus knowing that I would be seeing him in a few days. Finally, he returned from the field training also frustrated with his job and his boss. Both of us being upset, I suggested that we should attend church. Thomas agreed to go to church with me every Sunday if possible. We started going to a church on the base whose pastor was Baptist. Our differences became easier to deal with and also we made several friends from the church. It was one Sunday late December of 1986 when the pastor asked Thomas if he thought that I would interested in working with American wives in Korea. American wives needed a great deal of assistance from Korean. American wives needed help with Korean culture and get them settled in new environment. I was definitely interested, and if I got the job that would be a once in a lifetime opportunity. Also, I could learn more about American people and be very helpful to myself and others as well. I told Thomas I would take the job. I desperately wanted to do something normal.

Before the following Sunday, I received word through Thomas to see the pastor, having made arrangements for an interview at Camp Howze in the chapel. The interviewer was Mrs. Choe. Mrs. Choe was highly educated in the United States and was intelligent who spoke in addition to interviewing me. I was hired by her on the spot and she was also my supervisor. Mrs. Choe worked at the 8th Army Division in the USFK/EUSA Chapel in Young San Seoul Korea. After talking with her, I admired her and wanted to be like her. She was impressed with all the answers to her questions about my family life and she praised me for the life I had. I became an outreach family life program coordinator. When my interview ended, she introduced me to the American woman who would be my partner for the next several months. Her name was Elizabeth and her husband was stationed in the artillery division, which not far from the Camp Howze. Elizabeth and I were introduced to each other and I showed her where I lived. We planned on meeting the following week in Seoul Young San's 8th Army chapel.

The Family Life Program at Camp Howze was established to aid American wives coming to Korea to be with their spouse and adjusting to the different culture. On the other hand, Korean women who married American servicemen lives weren't easy either. Therefore, I found the resources for easy access to the camp for Korean wives. This work was educating Korean women for introduction to American culture, and to illustrate American cooking and teach English as a Second Language. Most of Korean women did not speak English; therefore, I formed a group of American and Korean wives together to share in American lifestyle and make life more enjoyable for both cultures. Furthermore, both culture's women could help each other when their husbands were in the field training. The purpose of the program was to acclimatize both wives to their new environment. The reason I was assigned to the Korean wives was because they were uneducated, had low self-esteem, and were uncomfortable outside their culture.

The worst part was that these wives had no intention of learning anything new. Therefore, whenever there was an American function to attend, their husbands had to be present, and the wives stayed home. My job was to help them become more self-reliant in their marriages. In their marriage, I was bridging the gap between each culture. This was extremely difficult because the Koreans resented the intrusion by outsiders. In Korean culture, the most demanding part of those women in their marriages was raising American babies. Most of the time, American husbands weren't present on a daily basis, and they were conflicted because of the Korean way of raising children. For example, most of the women constantly held their baby whether the baby cried or not. Then, when the husband came home after two or three weeks in the field training and wanted to spend time with his wife, his wife chose to be with the baby rather than the husband. Next, cooking was another big issue with these wives because they could not read the recipes. So I was there to encourage them to attend the American cooking classes and English classes as well on the base.

Elizabeth's job was the same as mine but she dealt with American wives. Every so often, she would find a few Korean wives and introduced me. We were a great team. Elizabeth and I would meet at least once a week and discuss our plans to contact as many wives as we could and survey what needed to be addressed in a monthly meeting. Then, we would have a monthly meeting in Young San Seoul with division coordinators. There were several divisions in Seoul Young San but Elizabeth and I were the best team out of all the divisions. We had the highest attendance in our program and the program was successful, because of our dedication, determination, and clear communication. We were actively providing what they needed and it was all about the timing of availability as a leaders. Elizabeth and I had the sense of enabling our gift to those wives in Korea.

Eventually, I started spending more time with the American wives because they lived closer to me than Elizabeth did. When the American wives came to Korea to visit their husbands, they were looking for an apartment outside of Camp Howze. In Camp Howze, word had been spread that I was a family program coordinator, and Thomas brought information to me about American wives looking for an apartment. I didn't speak well but I assisted them in renting an apartment, signing the contracts and so on, and let them settle in a new environment. This kind of work was rewarding because I liked to help people and it made me feel good. I felt that there was some kind of enjoyment. There was a group of three women who lived in one apartment. These women had many things to learn from me. I taught them how to change the charcoal in their room (if they did not change it every 6 hours, the flame would die and hard to get it going again).

Sometimes, one of them ran down to my home and asked me to help them. The charcoal had been dead for awhile and they did not know what to do themselves without my help, especially in winter. Finally, the warm weather had arrived. I took them to the market to shop. They loved the Korean market. It was very cheap but great quality, and all people were really good to the Americans. Some of them wanted to know how to cook Korean meals and I taught them a few things. I was enjoying hanging around these Americans and the first thing I noticed was that American wives were willing to learn the Korean way of life. As a result, it was a pleasure for me to work with them and I had the hands-on experience with the Americans. At this point, I realized how much I could learn from my experience with these American women. I also realized how sad it made me to see the unwillingness of the Korean women to learn and grow.

Through my efforts, I did run into some stubborn American men who did not want their wives to be educated. These men did not want to their wives to be like American women but I did not know what that meant. I believed this was cultural stupidity on both parts, and was the cause of many divorces between American servicemen and Korean women. It was a golden opportunity of a job, and I was preparing for my new life as an American wife in the United States. Unlike a lot of these Korean wives, I was in a situation where I would not be left behind in Korea, and I promised that I would be going to the United States with my husband. Thomas supported me with all his effort to make my job easier and because of him my job was successful.

Throughout this job experience, Elizabeth became my first and best American friend, both   professionally and also on a personal level. Occasionally, we spent time with her daughter, Mary, when she was about two years old. Elizabeth was a teacher so she helped with my English and sometimes just the two of us went shopping and did other things together. At about this time, I met another American wife who would become like a sister to me. Her name was Lisa and I met her on Sunday church service where Thomas and I attended. The pastor introduced us after Sunday church service and she was looking for an apartment. Elizabeth and I got together with Lisa and found her an apartment and got her settled in. Lisa was the wife of an officer and she volunteered her time to help us on when huge projects came up. She gathered a few of her friends who were also wives of officers involved in volunteering with our project. The first project was taking Korean orphans to the Children's Amusement Park in Seoul. We arranged transportation and lunch for everyone.

This was a wonderful trip because these children did not have the opportunity go anywhere or with someone who was willing to take them to see different things in Korea. It was a rough day, even fair weather but we had walked many miles and rode a few rides in the park. We had lunch and everyone had a wonderful time. The bus dropped the children to the orphanage and by the time we arrived at Camp Howze, we were totally exhausted.

The second outing was just for husbands and wives who were involved in the first project and it was to show our gratitude. We went to a Korean Folk Village. The theme of the Folk Village was a display of how Korean people lived thousands of years ago. In the Folk Village, employees dressed the way people used to, and they had basket weaving exhibits. People were squatting down for hours of labor weaving bamboo and some other materials. The Americans' eyes were lit up because they could not squat down like Koreans and they were amazed by how the Koreans sat. Another display showed an old classroom where children sat on the wood floor with chest high desk and ancient schoolbooks. In the temple, there were intricately carved dragons colorfully painted on the ceiling, and án altar, a beautiful gold Buddha was sitting gracefully watching our visit. In the village square, there were performers dressed in colorful folk garb and dancing to an ancient music created by handmade instruments. As the music played, there was a high wire performer who performed without a net.

By the time we were almost through all the exhibits, we were able to attend an actual ancient wedding ceremony. The bride was carried by four men in a carriage to the middle of the courtyard. A huge mat was on the ground and in the middle there was a table. On the table, there were displayed different kinds of rice cake which was colorful and with many different kinds of fruits. The bride and groom's sides had four people side-by-side. These people were to hold the bride's and groom's shoulders when they bowed to each other in front of the table. The bread makers from either side of the family would spread rice for them or tossed them dried olives for the bride to bear a son. The bride had to catch the dried olives. When the wedding ceremony was done, the groom would go with his friends and hang upside down by his feet on the ceiling and drink until he was drunk. In the meantime, the bride waited for the groom to return to the room. The bride would wear the heavy hair garment on her head and a Korean folk dress. When the groom was carried in by his friends in a drunken state the bride would spend the first night in her husband's home. In the room, when the candle was extinguished, the people would stand outside to watch from the door. They would poke a hole in the door because it would be wallpapered. It was Korean tradition and the reason behind it was because the bride and groom must be witnessed by people whether they had intercourse in order to have the next generation.

After this ceremony we also visited an ancient burial property of an important people, kings or queens. On the way out from the village square, we stopped at an ancient pub where drinks were homemade from rice wine, and tasted old fashioned Korean pancakes, which were made of mung beans. This trip fascinated all the Americans and everyone would remember the day as well spent in Korea.

Shortly after our Folk Village visit, I got a call from Elizabeth's husband, who said she was in the hospital. My husband and I visited her immediately in Young San 8th Army Hospital. She had severely injured her spine. Elizabeth had to be airlifted to a hospital in Texas. I cried when I saw her in the hospital bed and both of her legs were elevated and she seemed to be in great pain. We said tearful goodbyes and I didn't see her again or didn't hear from her for a long time. As we left the hospital, I thought about when we worked together, and in my ears I still heard the sound of her voice. She was calm, like a big sister tried making me understand what she was saying. If I did not understand what she needed to discuss with me, then she would bring an English dictionary and point out the words. It was easy for me to understand this way but nevertheless in our hearts we always knew what had to be done. Besides our professional relationship we were true friends and I knew we would meet again, some day, somewhere, only time would tell. When I came to the United States many years later, I received Christmas cards from her every year, and we were on the phone for an hour or two. She told me about how she was doing since she left Korea. She'd had surgery and was walking with cane for a long time. In the midst of battling with her health, she had another baby boy and was teaching again. We phoned a few times and I talked her about how my life had been changed. Elizabeth told me her daughter, Mary was in the college, and her husband was retired from Army and her son was in the high school. Her husband went back to the college and got a degree in business and was working for a private company. The last time I heard from her, she planned on living in a southern state. Her family bought a home then her family lived through Hurricane Katrina.

After Elizabeth left, the outreach program grant was not renewed but I continued to help Korean women if they needed me to help them. It was my duty or maybe I felt compassion for these women. This happened at an opportune time, as I was going to be shipped out with my husband. In the two years since I had gotten married, I realized many things had been changed inside of me but I could not communicate with Thomas. I had limitations of expressing my thoughts and feelings, and the only way I would dealt with it was forgetting about the importance of being me. I also learned that philosophically, no matter what language we spoke or what culture we were raised in, as long as we learned to get along with each other and try to understand the difference between all of us then I would be alright. It was my firm conclusion that I would not make any problems in my life. As I got closer to the American culture, I drifted away from my Korean heritage. I felt that I betrayed my culture, but it was far removed from who I was at that time and I meant to lived way I wanted. At this point I was an American living in a foreign country. From that day forward, every American I met they were my beautiful friends. My job had changed me into something more than I ever dreamed of. I felt encouraged and accepted by a higher class of people and I received the first compliment I ever heard in my life. Because of these positive, uplifting people in my life, I became able to leave my past behind forever.

Kateleen K. Washington

Eleven

My husband and I were to leave Korea on his birthday, July 7, 1987. I decided to throw him a birthday party on July 4th with all my dear American friends and their husbands. I had a group of officer's wives, Lisa, Sandra, and Lena. I invited one Korean family who lived behind us and the husband was Cleaby. Thomas' birthday party was at our home and I did not know how to get the word out to them. I told Thomas to let them know what time dinner was, and the theme of the occasion was goodbye to everyone but also thanks helping me in every way possible while I was working. Every one of them came for dinner and they loved my cooking and especially Lisa wanted to know how to make spinach. She said that she had only seen spinach in the United States in a box. I had blanched it a couple of minutes and it still had all the vitamins in it and also the crunch. I made the traditional Korean dishes and we had a cake. At the end of his birthday party, I told Thomas to wear a white scarf on his head and I gave my clip-on earrings to him so that I could take a picture of his happy face and the rest of my friends. It was the finest memory and I wanted to keep it in my heart. We exchanged gifts. Lisa gave me a Betty Crocker cookbook. These three women really thought about me and what I needed the most when I came to the United States.

I was truly happy for once in my life with my husband. I thought I was the luckiest woman in the world. Later that evening, we all went to the Camp Howze to watch the American 4th of July fireworks. Even though I did not know why they celebrated the 4th, I had a great time with my friends. Lisa sat behind me and Thomas was next to me, interpreting what Lisa was saying. Lisa and I were really good friends while we were in Korea, but that was about to change; but I just did not know how. I was inexperienced in human relationships when I was growing up and it was the most difficult challenge that I would face in the years ahead.

On the 10th of July 1987, my husband and I left Korea for good. We had already shipped our belongings to Army Base in Folk Polk, Louisiana; that was where Thomas would be stationed for two more years after his leave for a month's vacation. We had planned to have a formal wedding ceremony with his family in attendance. Mid-morning at the airport, Lisa was there to wish us well, and as we said good-bye to each other she promised to see us when she returned to the United States shortly after we left. I was torn apart, disheartened, and unstoppable tears streamed down my face like a waterfall. In that moment, all my past memories, both good and bad, flooded my mind and heart. I was sure I would never step on Korean soil again. I made a promise to myself that no matter what how difficult the future might be I would never revert to walking that path again. I wanted to find freedom and live life the way every human deserved. I felt the Land of Freedom the greatest country in the world would give me that freedom, and hope that my dream would never die.

Our bus took us to where we boarded our military transport. We flew to Japan and waited for a couple of hours where we caught the next flight. The Army airplane was full of soldiers. The plane seat was uncomfortable and it was hot. I began to ache in my body. Every joint was swollen and I did not know what to do. It was a miserable trip for some hours. Thomas looked at me for awhile and he asked, "Do you want to drink this whisky?" He gave me a sample bottle of whisky. I could not think of any other way in order to relax my aching body. I engulfed the whole bottle and slept through Japan to the United States. My joint aches was could have been caused by heat or the changes in climate, and my body was responding to it. When I woke up from whisky, it was humid, and my body was soaked from sweat but my ache had disappeared. The Army airplane brought us Oakland, California where I had to go through U.S. Customs. We did not have time to go outside of airport, but when the plane was in the air Thomas explained to me about Oakland, California and Salt Lake City.

We boarded the civilian flight TWC from Chicago to our final destination Metro Airport in Michigan. The trip took us 3,200 miles and a total of about 24 hours in the airplane. It was a long journey and while on the plane, I was really sick. I had to drink hard whiskey in order to continue the journey. All the joints of my body had swollen and it was really uncomfortable in the seat. However, we made it home safely and it was still the evening of July 10th in Michigan. At the airport, Thomas' oldest brother Eddie was waiting for us. When they saw each other, they exchanged a handshake and Eddie took us to Thomas' parent's home in Garden City, Michigan. I did not see anything while we were in the sky but it was alright because I did not miss much. The only one thing in my mind was, *I must survive and go to school. Everywhere I go, people are the same.* Unconsciously, I was already competing with Thomas, my husband, but I did not realize it many years later.

While we were in the car, I wanted to see outside but it was so dark I could not get a first impression of my surroundings. For all I knew there could have been rice patties alongside the road, or so I thought. When we drove up to the house, Thomas' mother was standing on the porch. I had seen a picture of her and her husband, but I did not realize how tall she was in real life. I stepped up to the porch and the first word she said to me, "You are very small." I smiled and she smiled back. She had a generous smile on her face and I was going to be all right. Then, she gave me a big hug. I felt awkward because I did not know what to do, especially I not what to say to her. I had never been hugged by anyone except a few people,

American friends in Korea and my husband. I kept silent because of my poor English. While I stood in the living room, her husband came in. Thomas' father seemed to be a tender-hearted person and Thomas looked just like him. Thomas' dad was a very quiet man but he stared at me for a long time because he had never seen an Asian woman before, I thought. I was getting uncomfortable and mom asked Thomas if he had supper. Finally, I was able to turn my head toward her kitchen and she asked me I wanted to have a sandwich. I said, "Yes." I was standing among these tall people; I felt like a midget and they were giants. We had been sitting on the couch for awhile. I sensed that Thomas was extremely loud talking about the time he was absent from home. I knew he was very happy to be home. I was too, but something started to bother me immensely and I shut my heart all at once.

They showed us our room upstairs and we retired because it was so late. During the night, I was awakened by a horrendous smell. This was a smell that I had never smelled in my entire life. In the middle of the night, I woke Thomas up and asked what the smell was. He said that it was a skunk digging through the garbage can on the street because the next day was the garbage pick up.

While we stayed with Thomas' parents about a week and a half, he took me to his friend's house in Detroit. The first time in this country I encountered a man other than my husband, Thomas. That particular day, a man was walking on the sidewalk in front of Thomas' old house. As we passed by, we looked at each other at the same time. He wore a beige jacket and had on blue jeans. He had clear deep blue eyes and blond hair. He had a muscular build, his face was pale, and he was a handsome man. Thomas said to him, "Hey, Man, how have you been?" They were hugged each and other people came out of from his old home and greeting with rest of his friends. According to Thomas, it was his old house which he bought it from his brother, Harold, and sold to his friend before he joined the Army. Thomas' friends were talking loud and giggling around the table by the kitchen. The kitchen wall was yellow, which was soaked with cigarette nicotine. The carpet was old brown, which matched the ceiling and the floor. They were drinking beers, smoking, and playing cards around the kitchen table. It was a familiar scene that I did not want to see ever again as long as I lived, but did Thomas know what I was thinking?

Everyone gave their names but I could not remember all of them, but one, his friend Kevin. His quietness stuck out like a sore thumb. It was a long hot summer and hours went by without my speaking. I sat quietly on the couch, and every once in a while Kevin's eyes and mine would meet. Each time that happened, we just glanced the other way. I remembered him many years later when we encountered again in a different place under different circumstances. I was fond of Thomas' friends. They were like children, optimistic, and playful and I adored them. Thomas told me that he liked his friends but sometimes he did not agree with those boys and that was because they were still children. Thomas had matured the time he was away from home and he got married and he had his career. Thomas had life plans but not his friends so he was a little disappointed in them. We returned after midnight and that was the one last time he played cards with his friends.

I had a real problem but I did not know how to quickly fix it. I hadn't eaten Korean food for a week and a half, and I was craving Korean food. I missed fresh food, something crunchy and hot. I asked Thomas if he could find an Asian market. He found a place in Ann Arbor. We bought a few things, and it brought home. What I made was different than what I had tasted in Korea. Then, Thomas took me to a grocery store and bought a jar of pickles. They tasted so good, and for a while I had a jar of pickles with every meal until we arrived at Fort Pork, Louisiana.

A week and a half flew by like a torpedo. We decided to hold our wedding ceremony in Grayling, in the northern part of Michigan, where Thomas' brother lived. Thomas had a large family, with six brothers and two sisters. They'd all gotten married or had extended families and children. Thomas' brother, Mick, had his wife Katie, and their two boys, David and Michael. The boys adored their favorite uncle Thomas and they hadn't seen their uncle for very long time and they had grown up. Mick took us fishing in a wildness with a soundless atmosphere, sandy ground and acres of ancient pine trees. I loved the place and I smelled the nature. I admired Mick's family. They were fortunate because they lived in the most beautiful place on earth.

Anytime when the boys saw their uncle, they were enjoyed talking to him; when this happened, I became a loner. I did not know how to make a friend and did not know how to talk to them. I thought to myself, *It will be temporary because we will be going home to Louisiana*. I found myself comforted by this thought. Mick's wife Katie had been my good friend since Thomas and I were together. She was an open-minded person but according to Thomas, they had marital problems for a long time. I did not quite understand what the story was but when Thomas said the word "Problem" I understood what he said to me.

While we were visiting Mick, we found a Methodist Church and made an appointment with a pastor. We looked at the church from the main street of the town; the building was pretty old and I felt that it was the one. The church was build from brick. We walked to the back of the church, and there was a flower garden which reminded me of a famous place in France. The path to the back door of the main church was placed in stepping stones. I loved the place. I knew we had found the right place. The main part of the inside church was magnificently beautiful with stained glass. I hadn't been in church since I arrived the United States and I hadn't seen inside of the church. The place was mesmerizing until this day. Finally, we sat down with the pastor and he explained to us what the day of our wedding procedures could be. He explained to us slowly because he realized that I did not understand each step of the wedding ceremony.

I asked Thomas' dad to give me away because I wanted to have my dad. Thomas' family became my family I never had, and I accepted it as part of my fate. We thanked the pastor planned on seeing him on the day of the ceremony.

Our visit turned into a family gathering within a few days but still more people would be coming for the wedding ceremony. I was overwhelmed by the large family and I felt that I was an outsider. The language barrier bothered me and I become much more quiet. I compared them to my own family. My family was very small at first then we were gone from the space of the earth. It got late and dark. Mick had an idea that he would take everyone piled in back of his pick up truck and just drive. We had ridden through the bumpy, swurvy and sandy Grayling road. While we were on the trail I saw my first porcupine on the road.

Thomas pointed out different things in the wild and taught me what those names were. At the same time I held tight on back of the truck because when we hit the bumpy part of the trail, my body jumped. It was fantastic! Mick's truck stopped at the Au Sable River bend and I saw the reflection of the first full moon in the river. The summer evening weather was cooling off faster than the city and I realized that I was a person who could not live without nature and nature became a part of me. This night was the first night for me to remember forever and I meant to remember as long as I lived.

The days were getting closer to the wedding; things became more hectic than usual. I had taken care of Thomas' suit and my wedding gown. We had our wedding rings but they would be taken care of by Harold's girlfriend. I remembered something Thomas asked me while we were in Korea. He wanted me to have a diamond ring but I refused because at that time we did not have money and we still didn't have money. I told him that diamond was just a rock, and our lives were better than a rock. As long as we had love for each other, we were stronger than a rock. Therefore, we planned on exchanging gold bands. It was a sweet and simple wedding but I hoped that it had meaningful depth and would be cherished forever.

On July 31, 1987, the day of our wedding, the rest of his family had arrived in Grayling a few hours before. Mick and Katie's house was full of family. I was upstairs and putting on make-up. Katie came upstairs and helped me my dress and veil. I could not believe that my wedding was really here. The day was a gray drizzly but I felt that my heart was tingling with excitement and adventure ahead. I did not fully realize that I got married until the wedding ceremony. At the ceremony, Thomas' dad walked me down the aisle. The minister asked, "Who gives this woman to groom?" And Thomas' dad said, "I do." We followed the minister's direction and made our vows to the family. Then minister introduced us to the family as husband and wife. We lit the candles and gave rings to each other. Then minister said, "Kiss the bride." We walked down the aisle. As we opened the front door of the church, the guests were throwing rice at us as we made out way to the Thomas' truck. I truly felt that I was his wife for rest of my life. When we arrived at Mick and Katie's, family was set up a food table for everyone. Harold's girlfriend, Jodi, had made a large sheet cake as a wedding gift. We cut the cake, and the first piece we had to share by feeding each other with our arms crossed.

There was quite a lot of things happening but I did not understand why we did what we did. The reason for the garter, throwing the bouquet, throwing the rice, and most of all, I did not understood the what the word "commitment" meant. After I changed my bridal gown we spent the night at the downtown hotel in Grayling. At the dinner, a musician played jazz and we ordered a special plate of all we could eat crab legs. I had the greatest dinner since we left Korea. On the table, piles of empty shells reminded me of little crab hills. In Korea, crab legs were very expensive and I could not afford to eat this much. After dinner, we slow danced to a real band and we went to the room.

We had a good night's sleep. Finally, we had relaxed without any concern, and tomorrow would be another day. We got up early next morning and planned on leaving Grayling, after seeing his brother Mick, Katie, and their two boys. The day began with a bright, gorgeous sunrise. We drove through downtown Grayling, and I looked closer at this town once more. The place reminded me of my country when Thomas and I were on the honeymoon. In the mist, I smelled the fresh pine trees and compared the countryside of Korea to the scenery of Grayling. As Thomas' blue pickup truck passed the Methodist Church, I asked him will he visit again. He promised me that he would when he got out of his duty.

We knocked on Mick's door; he was just waking up. I did not see Katie and according to Mick, she went to work and the boys were still sleeping soundly. Thomas went inside and good-bye to them. While Thomas was inside talking to the boys, Mick was outside and talked to me. He knew I did not understand English so he showed me in funny gestures of slapstick. He told me that if Thomas did not listen to what I said, I should be kicking him. I laughed and understood what he meant. I felt delighted, and I thought that I would be seeing them in a couple of years. While we were talking, Thomas came out and thanked him, and we hugged them good-bye. They did great things for our wedding and more. I was totally relying on Katie's support all the way until the end. It was a wonderful experience with the entire family, and the experience taught me that having a big family would be a fun. We were headed to Garden City and would spend less then a week before going to our temporary home in Louisiana.

On the road, Thomas explained to me about his brothers and sisters' different family situations to me, especially regarding Harold and Mick. Harold was going through a divorce. I told Thomas in broken English, if we ever had problems in our marriage, we would first discuss the problems. He said to me that if we had problems in our marriage, we should try three times before getting a divorce. Furthermore, he brought up Mick and Katie also and they had marital problems for a long time. It was three or four hours of driving and we arrived in Garden City in the afternoon. The day was August 1, 1987. We'd had dinner and were ready to go out and do something.

There was a phone call and Thomas picked up the phone. I saw Thomas' face became pale and extremely upset. His parents were out and we did not know where they were. Thomas hung up the phone and he told me that he needed to be alone for a while. He slammed the kitchen door and walked out. A couple of hours later, Thomas and Harold came to the door and so did his parents. All I could hear in their conversation was that Mick had been shot with his shotgun, and Mick's son David found him upstairs. David saw Mick's writing and his dad's splashed body. It was the most horrible thing I could remember but I had no idea what it was like for people to blow themselves away. I did not have the imagination about what that was like because I never was exposed to such death. The only time I did see this was in the movies but even then, Korean people never made gutsy films. I did not know what was really happening to Mick because no one explained it to me. The next morning, we all had to drive to Grayling and we met at the funeral home. There I realized that Mick had shot himself. I saw Katie was in tears. Thomas' parents were different from the day before, especially mom was the worst. It was August 2nd 1987. I did not have a chance to speak to Katie but even if I did, she would not understand a word I said. I know I told her that my mom died and I had her funeral. It was exactly the day of my mother's death; I'd had a wedding ceremony and my mother's funeral, and now Mick was having a funeral. What a coincidence but I did not have any consciousness whatsoever. From that day forward, all I remember about Mick was his suicide and Thomas never spoke to me about his brother ever. After the funeral, somehow I must have blocked out the memories of Mick's family.

Twelve

I really can't remember which day we left Michigan. The only memory I had was that it was the hottest summer in Michigan. The weather was scorching everyday 99 degrees and some days were over 100 degrees for a long time. Everyone's yard was brown grass instead of green. A few days before leaving Garden City, we received a call from Lisa. She was visiting her parents in Cincinnati, Ohio and we would be stopping at her parents. We were on the way to Louisiana. I was glad to see her in the United States; in this huge country I had a friend waiting for me. We crossed the Ohio River and her parents lived in a suburb of Cincinnati. We met Lisa's mom and dad and her huge cat. We were there for a few hours or maybe less because Thomas wanted to get back on the road as quickly as possible. We were just about to leave, when she said, "Kyong Mi, I will give you a new name. How about Kay, okay!" Lisa gave me a new name and I became "Kay." She said to me that my Korean name was really hard.

When we were crossing the bridge, it was horrendous evening traffic. I had never seen so many cars moving so slowly on the bridge. I guess that Thomas was used to driving those many hours while he was in Detroit. On the bridge, my eyes were busy looking around downtown Cincinnati and the bridge itself I'd seen in a War World II movie. We drove straight ahead and we came to Kentucky flatland. The only excitement in this state was miles and miles of farmland. The sun was setting to the west and my husband wanted to pass through the winding Ozark Mountains, almost like Sul Ak Mountain in Korea. In the rolling hills, steeply winding road and along the edge of the road, we were riding a roller coaster all the way through the Ozark Mountains. I remembered late night we stopped at one place and rested but I cannot remember in what state that was.

We drove two or three days to get to our destination, and the last day we did not stop. We finally arrived in Fort Polk, Louisiana. The sun began to rise and the weather was humid, even early in the morning. We could see red clay and swamp, and a tree standing like a ghost. Finally we were on the main road of Fort Polk and in the distance I saw the sign reading "Welcome." Along the both sides of the street were lights. He went to a building and signed in.

At first, we rented a house on off post because Army housing wasn't available right away and we had to wait for a certain period of time. We rented a house on the main road near by Fort Polk because it was easy for Thomas to go to work. Next to my house there was a Korean grocery store and that was perfect solution for me because I did not know how to drive. Our house was not built with brick so in the distance it looked like a brown shack. The color of the house was brown. There was sandy ground, and plenty of pine trees that gave us shade all day long. We lived in this house for about a year and in that time we had a marvelous life.

In those two years, I had dealt with loneliness also because I did not have a friend and it was a huge change in environment. Nevertheless, I would not exchange it for anything. It was the most precious time I had ever spent with my husband. Of course, we did not have much money to go anywhere, but we managed to spend a lot of time together. As usual, Thomas went to field trips every two weeks out of the month, and when he came back he wanted to go to fishing. When Thomas did have time off, we used to go to camping and fishing. We would get up around 4:00 a.m. and drive about two hours before the sunrise, and we fished from early spring to the around the Thanksgiving weekend. It was the most unforgettable experience, and the State of Louisiana was the place I called Fish Heaven. Every time we went fishing we caught at least 40 pounds of crab and shrimp. I had to practice how to throw the net. It was heavy but I learned quickly. Often, there was squid in the net; I was happy because Thomas did not like squid and it would be all mine. We were blessed. Every time we came home from fishing, a big cooler was filled with fish, shrimp, crabs and squids. What a place! I loved being outdoors with Thomas. He was a patient man and paid attention to me when we were out. We had fun.

Fall had passed and it was our first year in Louisiana. Nature brought for me the most magical moments that I never forgot. Thomas had said that on this side of the state people hardly ever saw snow or ice storms but that year we saw both. We went for a ride because it was such beautiful scenery along the country road. All the trees wore sparkling outfits and glittered like crystal jewels. Some of the branches were hanging low and were heavy. It was the most different image of tree I had ever seen in my entire life.

Thomas was basically a good and simple guy who did not make me do anything different but if I needed something more. I hardly ever asked for anything except about English grammar. We'd had fun but it was my time to do something for myself. I had not forgotten my long lasting goals, and I needed to work at it in order to succeed. I had someone whom I loved dearly and shared every single moment with, someone who gave me love, shelter, food . . . what else could I ask for? In my mind, all my dreams and sizzling ambitions would come true as long as I put my heart into everything I did. I had the opportunity to become anyone I wanted to be. It looked to be a long and hard battle, but I realized that I could not let anything stop me from doing what I wanted, even if something was in the way. When I was about nine years old, my education ended because of circumstances. Parents were supposed to support the child emotionally and give them opportunities to be self-sufficient. I had none of these. There was no food, scarce shelter and no school.

I was not hungry anymore, I had a roof over my head and someone always with me no matter what. But I was extremely lonely most of the time, and I had to live with it and accept my circumstances. Again and again, I made a promise to myself that I would become somebody someday. Loneliness permeated my whole being, and many nights I soaked my pillow with tears.

I wanted to be strong-minded, determined, and steadily working towards my goal so that I would have hope for the future. When I came to the United States, however, I was sick a lot; in the summer of 1988, I had a major problem in my woman's organ. I had such a headache that I had to go to an emergency room after midnight. Doctors did not figure out what it was. All of a sudden, I had a killer headache with bleeding in my underpants for several hours. No matter what I was made of. I think my sickness was from being isolated emotionally and physically, but also I had the feeling that I lost a baby because that bleeding wasn't a normal period. I felt that maybe it was meant for me not to have a baby. My husband provided me with everything I needed. I didn't have to work while he was in the Army, even in the United States at first. Maybe I'd needed those times to relax because just before I met Thomas, I was ready to give up my life and I needed a break and Thomas was my rescuer. I did not think at that time. I was beginning to complain about a lot of little things, around home and school.

Again, I took six different classes for a year's period of time: English as a Second Language, Reading, Business Math, Computers, Accounting, and Typing classes. It was hectic, even though I did not work. Consequently, Thomas gave up trying to teaching me because I was asking technical questions like English grammar and my husband and I argued a lot. I could sense a change in him and I couldn't ask him anymore about my homework. Our communication was at a standstill and moreover, I did not know how to drive for two years in Louisiana. I still didn't know the language well, but did not have problems getting around. I had such magnetism that I always had a lot of wonderful friends and teachers who did not mind helping me when my husband wasn't around. I had all good people around me but they were all temporary, and yet, I was thankful that I found the people when I needed them. On the other hand, I discovered that each state has some kind of program that provided for everyone who had a desire for achieving individual goals. Almost all teachers were trying to lead students to become better people through education. In addition, I learned that the majority of Americans had a good attitude toward themselves. Americans were easygoing people and they were happy people, and I liked the way of Americans even though it was different than when I experienced it in my country. It was my choice that no matter how hard it was; even if my husband wasn't with me, I had to push myself to the end.

In the late fall of 1988, at last, we moved into military housing. It had an upstairs and we resided in the upper level. It had a balcony, two bedrooms, bathroom, living room and a pretty good-sized kitchen. It had a lot of storage space. It was luxurious living and I just loved it. We had a couple of neighbors who could become friends and I also found a Korean woman friend, too. I was closed to our neighbor in the lower level. One day my neighbor asked me if I would like to take care of a cat. I'd never had a cat before but she took me to a place where many kittens waited to be adopted. I followed her and picked out a kitten. It had a gray stripe and green eyes. It was so tiny and hard to hold onto; I could have killed him if I was not careful. I brought the kitten home, and my neighbor gave me instructions on what to fed him and how.

A few days later my husband returned from field training. He walked in the door and said to me," I am dirty, sweaty, and smelly," and he was sat down to take off his boots. I still did not say anything about a kitten because it was a surprise and I wanted for him to find it in his own time. He was taking off his boots when he heard a squeaking sound. He'd asked me, "What was that?" The kitten came around him within a minute. He saw something coming toward him, wobbling around its body. It was too weak and small and did not know how to meow. The kitten began to sniff Thomas' dirty socks and he picked it up. I explained to him how I got the kitten and told him that the kitten needed a name. First thing he said to me was, "How about Willy?" Thomas thought that the kitten was weird because it sniffed his dirty socks. Willy became our companion and I took care of him like a baby. When Thomas was gone for a week or two, my school, housework and cat became my joy. Then when Thomas returned, we went fishing. We caught shrimp or fish and I gave Willy fresh shrimp and cooked fish for his meal. Willy became a huge cat but also he was very healthy cat. Thomas liked him also. He liked to play with the cat and sometimes he bit him a lot. Willy was my buddy and when the cat bit Thomas, he was really mean to him. I just did not like anyone hurting animals. Sometimes I got angry at Thomas because my cat could not speak and I felt that he was hurting me and I was emotional about it. Thomas used to tell me that my cat was tough and he would be fine.

We were really tight on our budget financially. The days passed by quickly and I wanted to work somewhere so that I could be helpful to my husband. I was concerned about being poor. Plus, all my life I'd spent money when I wanted to because I'd always earned my own. In marriage, however, I had to be careful because we were two people but only one worked. I did not like the way I felt. Then, someone told me about plasma donation, that it was safe, that a nurse took blood and would give me money. Since I never had experienced it, I wanted to know more about it. So I told Thomas and we went together. I made extra money.

I thought I could learn to drive from my husband. Well, it was the wrong decision on my part. I'd asked Thomas to teach me driving and he agreed. What a nightmare experience that was. I wasn't ready but through that driving experience, I found out what his personality was. He had a quick temper without patience. He tried to teach me how to drive but he did not know how to explain how the blue

141

pickup truck worked. The truck was a Dodge Ram, full sized with a manual stick shift. I had a hard time coordinating my arm and feet at the same time. His frustration finally got to him. He started using bad language and screamed a lot while I was in the driver's seat. As a result, my feet froze up and my arms were tired and I was nervous. I tried not to make a mistake because if I did, he yelled. I was scared of him in the truck and I gave up learning from him. I was sad. The man I married in Korea wasn't with me anymore. I began to wonder what it would be like if he got out of the military. I realized I should not make any problems because if I did our relationship would get worse. I stopped asking my husband to teach me to drive and in fact, I stopped asking anything of him.

At this point in my life, I just needed to be quiet. I was silent for all my life, and if I could be silent for a little longer I would be fine, and that was the only solution. I sealed my feelings for myself in order to not to be intimidated by my husband. He already knew I did not have self-esteem and I knew he would not teach me anymore. I began to look at my husband's face, and his expressions let me know what he was feeling; either he was angry, tired or frustrated. I could easily detect the problems and that was my pattern to stay out of the problems. All my life, I had learned from the street to conceal my feelings of hurt. I was used to living without affection and care; my relationship with my husband was not adequate but the marriage had to go on. I was not an educated person but I was experienced in life and that would keep me safely in the marriage.

Korean culture taught me those three different fundamental rules about how to become a good wife. These rules were: I should not talk for three years. I should be blind for three years, and I should not hear for three years, and if I live these nine years, everything should be fine. These golden rules were taught from generation to generation in order to become satisfied in family life and marriage. I became selfless and I had to, but did it work?

Thomas' military career had come to an end and he decided to go home. I guess that we weren't meant to be traveling all over the world. We knew we would be missing this state because we had such a great time in Louisiana; though the weather was hot and sticky, the fishing was great. On the way home, I asked Thomas what he was going to do besides working for his brother. He decided that he would also join the Michigan National Guard because he would be missing the Army. He also figured that unless I could get a job right away that was the only option for him. It was early February or March in 1989 when we arrived in Michigan. On the way to his parent's home, we saw the snow on the ground like a white patchwork. He said, "It is Michigan." I hadn't been seen snow for two years and I missed Korea. I was looking at the snow and was homesick. That time of year in Korea, people would freeze to death if they were outside. It was a brief moment and I drifted away from reality. Maybe I was daydreaming about Korea when my husband was talking to me. For awhile, I'd closed my eyes and wondered around in my head what it would be like if I was still in Korea. Thomas had said, "Hey, we are home."

We arrived at his mom and dad's. I brought in my buddy, Willy, and his mom said, "Oh, my God, he is a big cat." Thomas' parents were glad to see both of us in good health. I had been changed since they saw us about two years ago when they visited us in Louisiana. I spoke a little better and became used to being with his mom and dad. I got closer to his dad instead of his mom because no matter how good she was I did not like women, period. I was scared of all women and maybe it had something to do with my mom but I did not know what the problem was with me and women.

We had lunch together and Thomas and I went out to look for an apartment. I knew before we left Louisiana that Thomas had talked to his older brother for job. His brother owned the trucking company and Thomas had no problem finding a job and it was secure. According to Thomas, he used to work with his brother before he joined the Army. We found an apartment about two miles from his parents. Our apartment was on the upper lever and it was one of the older buildings in Westland. It was a great location and I could walk easily everywhere: Farmer Jack, 7-Eleven, and all kinds of little stores and a strip mall. I made an easy transition in a different environment. I was used to living on the Army base which was small, and compared to city living Thomas' parents were concerned about me. By the time we moved into the apartment, our furniture had arrived from Louisiana. I had a lot of work to do and Thomas had to go to work. He went to work around 7:00 a.m. and came home about 5 or 6:00 p.m. and we had a lot of time together, unless he was scheduled for National Guard training. At his work, his brother gave us a good health insurance and I wouldn't be suffering if I got get sick. Thomas' mom was closer to us and so often she would stop by and take me out for a ride.

I was doing alright but I wanted to have a job. I did not care about a good job but I wanted to work. I became bored with being home alone again. I did not like being home alone waiting for my husband to return. I wanted to go to school but it was very far to walk. Therefore, Thomas had to drive me to school after work, and wait for me after class. He could have been tired of caring for me but at the same time I did not waste my time. I read an exam book for getting a driving permit while I was in Louisiana and it was almost the same in Michigan. I brushed up for the test because it had two parts, a written test and the actual driving test. We had been in the apartment for several months. Thomas found a private driving school and I went out for a day. I did not like the instructor because he was yelling when I was on the wheel. I told my husband about what had happened. He fired him. Here we were, going through the same circumstances again and we had to start from the zero point. Finally, I found a job at a bakery and of course, it was walking distance which less than a mile one way. I started working right away. The bakery owner liked me and he was also a foreigner, and he was compassionate. I could take anything I wanted from the bakery after my work was done. I worked in the bakery for a year and a half.

Meantime, Thomas found another driving teacher. I already had a permit but I hadn't practiced driving. Thomas came from work and he said that he ran into his teacher who taught his driving lesson. He was his high school teacher and he was a super nice guy. Thomas made an appointment and the teacher came to pick me up. The teacher looked to have a really sharp and agitated personality. He was a small, bald man but when I sat on the driver seat next to him I certainly became a calm individual ready to tackle anything. I was not scared of the anyone on the road. He took me about two hours in traffic, and I took two lessons from him. At the end of the session he said to me, "Tell your husband that you will be a good driver, you just need to practice." Thomas' high school teacher called him in the evening and talked him. I did not know what he said to him but next thing I knew Thomas sold his blue pickup truck. The same night we bought a Jeep Cherokee. It had an automatic shift and 4x4 which I had no problem to drive. The color was between brown and deep orange and I began to practice with automatic shifting. I loved the Jeep.

I waited for winter to pass and the following spring I passed the driving test. My life suddenly became very hectic between work and school. Thomas was usually home alone. Our circumstances had changed but I did not forget a wife's duty. I went to work the same time as Thomas since I changed jobs. After I got home from work, I made dinner for my husband around 4:00 p.m. and I went to school. When Thomas came from work, the car was mine and I had some sort of freedom and a new experience I enjoyed enormously. Our circumstances were changed. It was my husband's turn to be alone. I was not aware that this was the beginning of our rocky marriage, and I was looking for something more than marriage itself. Our emotions were running high and so often our voices became high-pitched.

I was still attending Livonia Adult Education Center and still trying to pass the GED test but I failed. I was miserably frustrated with daily living. I was not moving fast enough, and the only hope I had was passing the test. In my life, whether I was in Korea or in the United States it was still the same and I got more depressed than ever. If there had been someone to tell me I was depressed and I probably could have thanked that person for reshaping my personality but unfortunately I had no one. My husband told me I would get it someday and his words made me angrier because what he said was neither encouraging nor comforting. Of course, I began to blame him for it even though it wasn't his fault. I thought that if he paid a little more attention to me I could have passed. He'd always said to me he loved me but I did not feel he loved me at all. My love was different than his. My idea of love was to walk with each other all the way to the end no matter what. I became silent again. Thomas knew that I was angry at the whole world. Therefore, he did bother me for awhile. I usually worked through my feelings alone because no one understood me, not even my husband. When I spoke, the words came from my heart and I acted upon the words. I knew that I was an odd person but I could not explain it to anyone and I was dying inside for a long time.

Thirteen

I was having such unsettling feelings but I did not stop trying again. I continued to attend English class the following semester. We lived in La Villa apartment for a year and it time for us to find another apartment. I had been in the United States for almost three years and we were going to move again. The River Bend Apartment had a pool and balcony upstairs. It had two bedrooms, a dining room, kitchen and huge living room. In addition, there were a lot of cabinets and the basement had a storage room also. We spent a little more money on rent but I liked it very much, and in fact, I changed my job to a vertical blind factory and worked 40 hours a week. It was the first decent job and I loved the money the factory paid me, but I had to work harder than at the bakery.

My job title was Packer. I packed the vertical blind rods, including hardware in a package. The company gave me a list of how many I had to pack per day. I worked really hard because I did not want to lose my job. The owner liked me because he knew Korean people worked honestly without making any problems. There were many Americans also but they complained about every little thing and about how the owner treated their employees. This company had no union or benefits, medical or any other types of insurance for employees. At work, I had to carry many packages of heavy blinds but my husband had great health insurance so I did not worry about anything. I noticed that everywhere I went, there were a few people always bitching about something and I did not like it because these people told me, "Aren't you lucky, you have a husband who can provide you with everything." They had no idea. I truly experienced some small-minded people in the factory. They did not understand why I was going to school. I didn't talk to them unless I had to. They saw me as aloof and maybe arrogant. I was fine with whatever people judged me—I did not care. As long as someone signed a check for me, that was it.

Certainly, my perspective in life was interesting and mysterious. I worked for several months in the factory. The factory owner hired the new supervisor, and I became his buddy. He was counting on my department production alone and if the production went beyond what he expected his job was secure. The company was making a lot of money. I packed 200-300 rods a day. According to a source, no one ever packed like me. When the slow time of the season came, we usually got laid off, but I never did. The owner laid off other people and called me to come to work. I was a really tough person and I survived in the factory.

I had every Saturday and Sunday off for fishing again. Thus, my husband and I found a different kind of enjoyment for fishing. We liked to go to fishing in Manistee Michigan for brown trout and salmon. Even once a year, we went out with a charter boat on Lake Michigan and the Manistee River. I became a happy person again just seeing the water and the majestic nature made me feel lifted from the congested city. The blind factory and school became less important. I had to focus on me. Thomas may have thought that I was selfish but I did not want to angry at the world anymore. I wanted to enjoy the moment when we were outdoors.

During the summer, I did not attend class but in the early fall of 1990, I went back to class again. All teachers were worried about me because I was a good student but I had spent some time to work harder in order to pass the GED test. They encouraged me that I was smart but the real problem was the language barrier. One teacher said to me, "Do not rush. Everything has its own time" and she told me to have patience. I knew I heard this before somewhere but I forgot. Absolutely, she was right, and under all the teachers' care I began to get a grip on myself.

In the second week of class, I met a male tutor. He was a substitute tutor for the next several months, and he would help me when I needed it. He then told me about himself and explained to me what his career was. His name was Mark, and he was a photographer who worked in the hospital. He had an interesting career and right away I admired him. He was done talking to me so I introduced myself very briefly. He listened carefully to what I had to say and gave me a class assignment which I had never thought about all my life until I met him.

The assignment was to write about one of the most important events when I was growing up in my own country. Suddenly, my heart became heavy and I did not know what to write about because I did not remember an event. Specifically, I did not remember my father at all. I was agitated and somewhat embarrassed. The story I'd kept in my heart for a reason was instead going out onto paper; it was hard. That night I just wanted to remember about my father and then it came to me. It was only once, but I had a beautiful memory of my dad and I finally finished writing it. While Mark was reading, he had a lot of questions about me. So I told him everything I had in my memory. He was delighted to hear about my story and I did like the tutor.

After class on my way home, I thought about my husband. Why did my husband never ask me about my past? I could have told him about it but all these years he'd never asked me. *Why?* It was a strange puzzle to me but I did not want to make a big deal about it. I thought that maybe he would ask me someday, when I spoke better English.

When I returned home from school, there was a familiar person sitting on the balcony with my husband. Thomas said, "Do you remember him?" "Yes," I'd said, "I met him when I came to the

United States house in Detroit." Kevin said, "How are you, Kay?"

Before I had a chance to speak to Kevin, Thomas told him that I was coming from English class and that I was doing super. This was the second encounter with Kevin and I felt so awkward. I did not know why but within a few hours, from school to home something really strange things were happening. I nodded slightly to Kevin and went into the room and changed. By the time I came out from my room, my friend came over from work. Her name was Young and she was Korean and worked with me in the factory. Actually, Young got me the job in the factory. I met her at our previous apartment and we became friends. She too, was married to an American and had two kids. She was seldom seeing her kids because her ex-husband took her rights and she was paying child support. She had been working very hard paying child support and taking care of herself. She was tight with money and asked me about being a roommate. Thomas and I talked things over and we decided we wanted to have a roommate. We also needed money and she could save money if we took her in. Kevin and Young introduced themselves and she went into her room. Kevin and Thomas continued their conversation on the balcony. Kevin was wearing a white tank top and white shorts. They were catching up with what had been going on in their lives. I remembered that Kevin was going to college and he would become a commercial artist when he graduated from Oakland Community College. I was stunned again because both my tutor and Kevin were artists. I did not know what the coincidence was but I couldn't connect the dots. That night Kevin left and I didn't see him again until a few years later.

The time went by quickly and Thomas was done with National Guard duty. It was the second time I met with my tutor, Mark. He asked me again to write about what it was like growing up in Korea. This time my thoughts went back to what I had in my life before I married an American. My thoughts traveled to the very beginning, when I was nine years old through thirteen years old. All those years

I hid away in my heart. All the bad memories were brought back to the surface. I was almost done with the semester and soon it would be Christmas. I was looking forward to seeing the holiday season. I told Thomas that this Christmas I wanted to have a real Christmas tree; it would be the first time I would have a real tree. I felt like a child and I could have a good dream like a child this holiday season. I wanted to brighten up my feelings and my husband's, too.

At this time, we were having major marital problems. In addition, I had my own pain and suffering from the past of which my husband was unaware of. Moreover, I had a physical pain that meant I could not always do as my husband wished. No matter how painful, however, I had to suppress my feelings and be silent because I was being noble to my husband. Finally, I told my husband that it was time for me to get a check-up with the OB/GYN doctor. I told Thomas that I did not feel anything except hurt. He wanted to know how he could make me happy till he was blue in the face but I had no answer to the problem in my body. The most important part of marriage was failing and I mentioned this to him many times. I told him about the first time in the United States in his parent's home; we'd made love in the middle of the night. I'd wanted him every time he touched me back then. Then, on the way to Louisiana in the motel and that was it. I wanted to feel again like that again. After those times, I did not feel anything when he made love to me. There was a changing in my physical self but also an emotional change, which Thomas had been ignoring consistently for long enough.

Thomas made the appointment for the special doctor. The doctor ordered a biopsy on an ovary and other kinds of tests. It was one after another, horrendous challenges in my life, but I was glad it was me. I thought that if Thomas had gone through what I was going through every day, what I could have done for him? In that sense, I was the lucky one. Finally, the doctor wanted to talk with both of us. We made another appointment and sat in the doctor's office. I did not know what doctor was talking about. I only knew I was going to have surgery within six months. Thomas explained to me that I would not have a child because I had enormous scar tissue covering on ovary and the sperm could not pass through the tube.

Of course, I didn't expect to have a child. That was one promise that I made myself firmly. My heart was set that if I could not take care of a child there was no plan for me to bring a child into the world. It was my firm decision when I was in Korea at a very young age. Then, when I got married every so often I thought about a baby but I did not mention it to Thomas. We left the doctor's office. It was time for us to move again to a different apartment because our lease was up. We had been moving every year and I did not like it.

During that time I had many disturbing dreams that were so vivid I remember most of them clearly to this day. It could have been another warning from my mother but most of the time I ignored it. My mother had been in my dreams for some reason but in times like this she came to visit me often. *I was in a house somewhere around a lake, up on the hills. The house was pretty big sized and it had an upstairs, but there was no light. I did not see furniture anywhere in the home but in the living room there was something old but I could not tell what it was. I scanned the area then went upstairs. Raindrops were falling from the eaves and I was standing by the window, sadly looking down at the lake. All of sudden, there was a change in the weather and the lake swelled up. It was windy and the wind picked up the water on the lake and it pushed the water up closer to the land. The home I was in was safe but the water was a dark forest green, which it reflected in the sky. I could not remember who else was with me in the house. There was someone with me but this person did not show his face. Then next thing I noticed, I was standing on the hill, in front of the home alone. My eyes gazed in front of the lake and I saw my mom walking toward the hill where I was standing. Behind her, I could see the swollen lake which could swallow her at any second. I didn't think she would care about whether she would be in danger. She was still walking toward me without a smile on her face. Her facial expression was sadness showing the agony of her life I used to remember. She was wearing her favorite Korean folk dress which was made of silk and the color was deep orange. As she rambled toward where I stood I recognized that her feet were in the mud.* I was waking up with tears again.

I shook my head and began the day with sadness in my heart. It was late 1991 I had been sleeping quietly many decades without any emotional support; I needed it more than anyone and yet I never received it from anyone, even my husband. My heart was stirred up much worse and I had nowhere to turn. Every so often, I talked to Thomas' mom but did she know what I was saying to her. Everyone pretty much could care less about me because they were in their own safe cocoons. There I was again asking someone to look at me. In my deepest heart I was screaming for help. "Let me out of here, where I can see the light. I want to be a happy person." I was in the abyss but in reality no one could tell because I was wearing a mask. I accepted who I was and became numb. How awful, living like this? I was a good person but I did not recognize myself. I was a prisoner of my past and present but swaggering through each day without knowing where would be a finish line.

Fourteen

In our lives, a majority of events took place in 1992. That was the year everything had been completed, one way or another. Thomas may have known our marriage was on the cliff because he was more aware than I was. I was a walking zombie who began to accept things the way they were. My surgery was set for December of 1992 and we decided to spend some time living a normal life. We decided to do something adventurous so we packed up and went north again for fishing. We did not have much money but we always did things when we needed to. I guess that the famous quote: "When we have a need, the universe will provide" is true. I felt really good but also I was thinking that if the surgery went wrong I would be much happier. My husband would sad but he would get over it soon enough. I was thinking devilishly because it started to seem to me Korea was a simpler life than in the United States. I wanted to live but I did not know how.

We never came back from fishing in Manistee with an empty cooler. Thomas decided that he would mount the huge salmon we'd caught together; it was his trophy and he wanted to keep it. I let him. It would be a lot of money to mount the fish but he deserved it. We were always generous with money even though we did not have much. It was our nature and we could not change. We did not save a lot but also we didn't owe anyone. We came back to the motel and went out for dinner and walked around the harbor edge of Lake Michigan. We were out in the boat on the water many times before, but standing on the land and looking out on the horizon, where the sky meets the water, was a spectacle. Then the sunset added colors that made the moment perfect. I wanted to stay in that moment forever. I touched white sand and walked along the beach. We would be fishing one more day and we would be coming home. We would not be sure when we'd be back again.

On the way home, he stopped by a trucking company in Manistee. The company was like his brother's place and Thomas knew these people. He went in and talked to them. When he came back to the car I suggested to him, "Why not open your own business?" Thomas took my suggestion. Our lives became joyous and somehow he found two partners. I did not know all the details about how they opened his business. He took on three partners from his brother's place. Thomas was the salesperson; two others re-built old truck parts, hydraulics, engines, (who knew what else they built?) but they were slowly improving themselves.

Thomas' business got better and he was a very busy person. Business was easy for him because he knew of many companies before he got out of his brother's place. I was working in the office with one of his partners' wives. She became the office manager and worked with me a couple days of a week cleaning the building. I still kept my factory job but I also knew how to sew. I learned different skills because the more I knew how to do things, at least I didn't get laid off. It was for the rainy days and I kept up with their demand. I was still going to adult education in Livonia, working in the office, my job, and taking care of home and my husband. I had excessive energy. I lost myself in the place of the unknown and I devoted myself to my husband.

On the other hand, I was dying every day without realizing it. I was a fragile soul who had patience, commitment, and love. All my life I was a natural giver. I had never taken anything from anyone until this day. Why? Because Thomas brought me into this country, and he paid me $2,000 to get me out of the slums. I should have been

155

happy but why wasn't I? I shut down my feelings completely with Thomas. Sometimes, Thomas wanted to be intimate but I rejected him many times. He had been gone for so long since he opened his business, and both of us become numb to each other. One of the big problems was I'd rather talk with the four walls.

It had been three months since Thomas had opened his business. It was really tight because he did not bring his paycheck and we were struggling to make ends meet, plus I had that appointment for surgery. I was sick of worrying about everything and the only way to escape was not waking up from the surgery table. *How cool would it be if that could happen to me?* It was my beautiful thought, and I was creating how I was going to die. I called the land of no pain and no worries "heaven." By the time the day was set for me to go to the hospital, Thomas brought a first paycheck. We went out to dinner with his partners to a Mexican restaurant and celebrated what had been accomplished. I did not have to worry about Thomas any more and I was ready for the surgery.

It was December 5, 1992 and what a miserable year it had been. On the way to the hospital Thomas was quiet and so was I. I prayed I would not get up. I asked God to take me. I was begging Him to take away my pain forever. I was looking for a way out. I did not know how long I went through surgery, and when I woke up from the anesthesia the pain was worse than I had ever imagined. Thomas was right by me and soon the doctor came to see me. He said that it was worse when he went in. The scar tissue was plastered over all parts of the ovary. He went on to say that he saved one ovary. He explained further that one ovary would make what I needed in ordered to function. I was 35 years old and still young it was not a good idea taking estrogen pills. The doctor was a Middle Easterner. Thomas liked the way he cared about his patients.

I was in the hospital bed for a week. Thomas' mom came to see me every other day and Thomas came to see me after work. Thomas looked awful but he did not say anything to me about what was going on. I thought that he did not want to worry me; therefore he did not say anything when I was in the hospital. I was ready to go home and Thomas' mom came to pick me up. I was coming home but I was not happy at all and in fact, I was terribly depressed. I came home and I could not work for two more weeks; no heavy lifting until the stitch on my belly healed.

The weather was still freezing cold and I could not do anything, but at least we were together on this holiday season. Thomas told me that something happened while I was in the hospital. Thomas then went to see a doctor because he had chest pains and took many tests. He came home and since then he felt awful but he did not know what was bothering him. The day after Christmas he went to see the doctor in the middle of the night. He asked me go with him. The doctor did not catch he had a collapsed lung the first time. The doctor thought that he had a cold.

Thomas was in the hospital for a week, then came home. I told him not to smoke and I was worried about him. Nevertheless, within two weeks he went back to the hospital for another two weeks this time. I told him smoking does not help getting better but he had to do what he had to and he was stubborn like me. We'd had problems in our marriage for a very long time but while we were together I did what I had to do. I was drifting away from Thomas, but also, I was expecting something to change.

It was the beginning of January 1993 and I went back to work. The only thing on my mind was making money. Thomas had opened his business a few months prior and he had been out of work and I was away from work. I borrowed money from my mother-in-law, $500, and I wanted to pay it back to her within a month. I was terrified after Thomas went into the hospital a second time. *If something happened to Thomas*, I'd thought, *how could I survive in this country?* I had too many negative thoughts pulling me away in many different directions and my work was my savior from going crazy. It was winter therefore, there wasn't much work and many employees had been laid off but the supervisor called me to work.

My work demanded so much: sewing, packing, and cutting the plastic materials. I did everything I could. The factory always had what they wanted as long as I worked. I was working hard and it made my surgery scar hurt more than ever. All day long I had to use a sewing machine pedal, sitting on the chair. Every so often I had to stand up to stretch my back. After work I went to see my husband in the hospital and soon he would be home, too. It was late January or early February and I needed money from the cash machine. I parked my car at the corner of Westland and Merriman Roads. I got some money from the cash machine, and I was ready to get into my car when I met Kevin at the street corner. This was the third time we encountered each other. He was Thomas' friend but it seemed to me he and I had some kind of string that kept on tightening. Mysteriously, we were getting closer each time we met. At this moment, I was stunned and thought, *What a strange meeting.*

I knew this time I could speak to him, so I called out his name. He remembered me and asked me about how I had been and about Thomas. I told him the latest news in our crazy life. He was concerned about his friend's health, and I told him to come by if he had a chance. I gave him our phone number. I came home and told my husband whom I met. A couple days after there was a phone call and it was Kevin. I told Thomas to invite him for dinner. After that day, Thomas and Kevin became closer than ever before, and we saw him frequently. Whatever was going on in our lives began to diminish slowly, and Kevin invited us to his graduation party.

In the spring of 1993, Thomas' health was great and so was mine. His business was booming and we had no money problems. All my worries and crazy thoughts were hidden away, and once more I was happy again. The three of us, Kevin, Thomas and I, did everything together. I never had this kind of experience with my husband and it was wonderful that Thomas had a friend like that. One time Thomas told me that he did not like his friends because they were still the children and how wrong Thomas was. I had many experiences with people but not real good people experiences with anyone before Thomas, then Kevin. Kevin did not miss hardly any week being together with us. We went to most sporting events together: baseball at Tiger Stadium, Red Wings games at Joe Louis Arena in Detroit. Then every so often on Sunday morning, we went bowling together and Kevin taught me how to bowl. Kevin did not know how to fish before he met us and Thomas taught him how to catch brown trout. He caught three brown trout and the biggest one was 13 inches. Afterward, we came to his home and cooked on the grill for supper. With Kevin, we could have many different things to do without spending a lot of money. I liked him very much and he loved me as a good friend. We shared things and we were honestly respecting each other. Having a friend like him was like having a brother which I had never had.

Through Kevin, I was discovering new possibilities of life, and beginning to shape parts of my personality that I had never known. He was soft-spoken, a tender personality. He wasn't an ordinary person. I did not understand why I felt like I did with him. Kevin was definitely different than Thomas. I had known Kevin for three months but I felt that I knew him a thousand years ago and I had an unusual attachment with him quickly. For me, Kevin was the rain and I was a dying plant waiting for the rain to come.

It was July of 1993. Thomas' business was doing great and he was really happy. When Kevin wanted to do something, he always had a raincheck with Thomas preceding any plan. Then Thomas told me what we would be doing together. We had a mutual understanding and respect for each other. Kevin asked us to go Pine Knob to see Santana. I screamed because I wanted to go. I'd heard his songs but I had never been to a concert before. We were at Pine Knob on the hill, on the lawn. Thomas warned me about rain but if it rained, it would be better. I loved the rain. Of course I had to have mosquito spray because those insects loved my blood. When we arrived at

Pine Knob, the lawn was already filled with the audience. We had fun! This was all new to me and I wasn't embarrassed by anyone. I danced. I hummed the tunes. Thomas hadn't seen me like that before. I did not drink and yet, I could have fun naturally.

We then went to Canada to see Cheap Trick. I did not know these musicians and I began to like them. Thomas loved listening to heavy metal (Metallica) and rock/pop (Chicago), and much more. On the other hand, Kevin liked listening to the opposite of Thomas, quiet and yet, strong expressive emotion (Paul Weller, Sade, and Peter Murphy). Thomas and Kevin were different but they got along well even though I was in the middle. I thought that they had a bond when they were young, despite their differences. In truth, I was pushing Thomas to be with someone other than me if he let me do the things I desired. I was in the box of marriage and I needed to breathe, and I needed to fly. I was the person needing to have freedom and Thomas had locked me up and I'd let it happen.

With Kevin, I wanted to achieve the many things I'd wanted for myself. I'd passed the driving test and yet, I was not comfortable driving without Thomas. I asked Kevin to go with me on the freeway driving. I had never been on the freeway because Thomas wouldn't let me. He agreed, and we went out on the freeway. The first thing he said to me was, "Don't be afraid. Do not worry about anybody or any other car. Keep your eyes on the road at all times and relax." He encouraged me and made me feel comfortable while on the freeway. I drove I-94 through all that traffic without fear. Actually, I was a confident driver who listened to music. My head was on the headrest, and one arm was leaning on the window, and I could talk to him all the way to our next stop. We stopped at the park in the City of Westland. We were sitting on the bench and he began to teach me about history. Kevin was my partner because I planned on taking the American Citizenship test. Kevin was testing me at the park bench and I passed it. I practiced the test for next year. I could have gotten my citizenship but immigrant law had been changed when President

Reagan was in the White House. I had to wait for six years and then, Thomas had to make an appointment with the American Embassy. I then took the real test and passed. I become an American Citizen. There were at least 30-40 people becoming American citizens and they would be living American dreams. All people must work hard in order to make it in this country. I had already experienced many cases of prejudice in Kevin's city but I did not know what prejudice was at the time. I am happy with the result.

I was thankful that I could learn much from Kevin and also I could talk to him about anything. I trusted Kevin more than my husband. I wasn't scared of Kevin because he never lost his temper. He always had his smile and it made me feel that I wanted to be with him all the time. Truthfully, he was becoming my only friend.

It was late August. I went to see a psychologist. I knew I had fallen in love with Kevin but I was not sure what love was. The doctor was Korean and he heard what I was saying and he put me on medication and sent me to a psychiatric hospital. The doctor thought that I had symptoms of suicide. I went in for two weeks. My husband and Kevin visited me at the hospital and he was very concerned about me. Both of them had no idea why I was depressed. The answer was simple but I couldn't express my feelings toward Kevin. I felt that I wanted to get away from Thomas because my inner conflict was draining the sap out of my whole being. At the hospital, Kevin tried to make me laugh but I could not. He grabbed a ping pong ball, rocket and asked me to play with him. He was a beautiful man. He cared about his friend and he wanted to rescue her before sinking to the bottom. I went along with Kevin. He cheered me up and eventually made me laugh. Whatever he did, it worked.

Slowly I got better and was soon able to return home. Kevin still visited us as a good friend. Then, in the late fall of 1993 Thomas and I went on a fishing trip up north. On the way, I asked him if Kevin could be my tutor. Thomas did not like teaching me at all but if I asked what I wanted to he usually let me. He said that it was alright

161

with him if Kevin agreed. I was nervous about asking Kevin to be my tutor but I managed to have courage and asked him. His question was why did I choose him. I told him the truth about Thomas, that he was not willing to help me. However, the reason I selected him was that he had great patience. I needed someone who had patience but also a compassionate personality. I experienced Kevin's kindness at the hospital, at driving lessons and many other times. Furthermore, he was an art teacher at the college, and I knew he had the tools to teach me. We decided on one condition we were to be tutor and student, nothing more. Kevin told me flat out that he didn't want to be a part of our marriage. He was a mediator who helped me and my husband's good friend, and he didn't want our friendship to end. We agreed, and so did Thomas. We arranged to meet at the Garden City Public Library once a week after his work. He had job as a commercial artist in Troy and he did freelance work. I, on the other hand, signed up for the fall term GED class through Livonia Adult Education.

Kevin was determined for me to do well in the class. Because he was a college teacher he knew what I was going through as a student. Every week we met; we'd go to dinner first and then to the library. Every week I was with him and my emotional struggle was difficult. He taught me as best he could. I was getting better and better at reading, speaking and comprehension. During this time, I wrote an essay with the topic "My Greatest Struggle Entering the United States." He helped me with the writing and he discovered a little about me from what I wrote. Sometimes, I saw him really tired but he never frowned. His teaching was an ongoing job without compensation. There was a great bond building and I respected him. Above all, most of time he could not understand what I was saying in writing but he never discouraged me or shut me out. He tutored me in every subject I needed to learn, and he made sure that I understood. He never made me feel less than a person, especially when we were having fun. He was like a father type. He stood next to me and showed me any new thing I had to learn. To Kevin, I was a little kid that was just learning to walk and talk. He was always there to teach me and that was his purpose. Throughout the winter, he taught me the GED and we brushed up on the citizenship test. I put Kevin on a pedestal and he deserved it. In fact, I learned more from him than I had from my husband in nine years.

In December of 1993, Kevin brought us a Christmas present. I opened and it was an image of fisherman. He had drawn an image of Thomas, the fisherman. In the image Thomas looked rugged and ambitious. Kevin's drawing described my husband perfectly and I liked his art. We thanked him and he kissed me on my cheek. I saw his face grow red and my face was also hot because of his sudden action. I never had anyone kiss me on my cheek and it made me feel something special. In my heart something had been changing since I met Kevin but I really did not know what that was. Sometimes I thought about it what love really was and I was confused with my husband; in my heart, I felt that it was the beginning of my new life.

The next few days we still saw each other, and Kevin invited us go his friend's New Year's Eve Party. Kevin was always quiet and shy if there were a lot of friends even though he knew all of them. As usual, Thomas was busy talking with the others at the party about his business, and how it had been doing well. There I was again alone and speechless. This time, however, Kevin brought a drink for me. I thanked him. I thought he was going to be with his friends. What a surprise! He sat beside me and we talked to each other. I did not know if Thomas noticed or not. I realized I wanted Kevin, but we kissed each other's cheek again, like friends. As the midnight approached, everyone blew loud whistles for the coming year of 1994. Kevin hugged me, saying "Happy New Year," and Thomas came and gave me a hug and we kissed.

We arrived at home around 2:00 a.m. I was on break from school and I did not have a job: I had to quit because someone threatened me with a razor blade. At the factory, everyone knew I had a husband who owned a business, and yet, I had never stopped working. A man from a different department came to me saying what I was going to do with all the money I was making? His tone of voice bothered me. I snapped. "Why do you have interest in how much money I'm making?" I shouted. Then, he went on and on . . . I was angry and told him get away from me. Then he was holding a blade and said, "I will cut you." That afternoon, my work was done. I came home and waited for Thomas' return and we went straight to the police station and reported what he told me. At the factory, he was a black man and he was in the Army like my husband. He knew what it was like with Korean women. At the factory I did not talk much but there was another Korean woman, who was my roommate in the past and she and I were like a cat and dog. We had not talked to each other for years. So whatever he had heard from people, he was joking around in my area and harassed me many times. I usually took whatever people said but this time I was out of control, losing my coolness. I guess that it was my time to move on and look for something else.

Between January and February, we did not do much because Kevin did not like cold, but Thomas and I enjoyed ice fishing. We went to Manistee for winter steelhead fishing and we did not catch a lot either. Fishing was our major hobby and I did mind at all. I loved to sit on the ice 10-15 degrees below zero all day long. Other than fishing, Thomas hadn't shown me any new hobbies. Since the New Year's party, Kevin and I were apart because I did not have class anymore and he was busy working freelance at home. Every so often he called us to go to bowling, and another time, three of us went to a concert in downtown Detroit. It was a huge bar and the musician was Paul Weller from England. He wasn't popular in this country but when we were in the bar, the place was filled with his fans. I loved his songs because it was a mixture of jazz and rock. I was listening to his song very close because his voice gripped strongly. Almost all of his songs were dark and it seemed to me he carried this in his heart; therefore, I was hooked on all of his albums. At the concert, the first time since I got married, I got drunk. That night I gulped down hard liquor while they drank beers. The weather was still cold but in no time, spring would arrive and we would be doing things together again. We were coming home and Kevin was driving because Thomas was drunk too. In the car, Kevin wanted to know why I was drinking so much. I didn't have answer for that. I just wanted to drink without reason. I was in a prison without guilt or maybe I was guilty because Thomas paid me money to get out of Korea. Emotionally, I was a mess. The man I'd married did not know what was wrong and the other man I cared about more than I should. It seemed to me life was a mess but love was something else and I could not say anything to either of them. Kevin was just a good friend and we had promised to keep our friendship.

Fifteen

Nevertheless, the spring had arrived. It was March of 1994; we bought a white brick house in Garden City. It had a detached garage and pretty good-sized yard, in the front and back of the new home. I remembered that while I was in the crazy hospital, Thomas wanted to buy a house with or without me and he did it. He did not need my help anymore. Thomas had an attitude. He was hiding his feelings about what he wanted from me and he got worse after he opened his business.

We were planning on moving pretty soon, and Kevin showed up to start helping us whenever he could find time. House painting, moving furniture and anything that Thomas needed help with. Kevin was peaceful with a lovable nature. We were settled in the new place and I found a new job. I was working at a promotional company on 15 mile and Telegraph Road. I drove in the morning rush hours for five days a week, and I was a shipping and receiving manager at a small private company. My duties were to ship out lab coats, golf T-shirts, umbrellas, and glasses. Whatever any other company wanted their logo on, this company carried it. At work, I was busy all day long. I had a great time at that company because my skill level was higher without the GED Certificate or high school diploma. The time came when I had to answer the phone and do computer work also. I could go to school no longer because I failed the GED test again, even with all the effort I got from Kevin. I was terribly embarrassed. I felt that I was dumb so I told Kevin how sorry I was.

He said, "Next time, don't give up." I was relieved because I found a job. Since my company needed an artist I introduced Kevin to them. I did not know Kevin ever got work from my company, but sometimes, Kevin came to my workplace and picked me up and we would go to the park. My husband could not pick me up some days and if that happened Kevin would. I used to have a car while I was working at the factory but I think we sold it.

Summer had arrived for more fishing. Thomas found the place in downtown Rochester, Paint Creek Trail. The three of us fished in the creek upstream and we caught a lot of brown trout and sometimes, there was rainbow trout. We all had waders and booths. When I went upstream I usually fell behind. I had chronic problems with balancing when I walked. Besides, walking in the water and beating the current were the most difficult things; under the water there were slippery rocks in the creek. Thomas was always ahead of me and Kevin was behind me. He simply cared about a woman in the water because he knew I had a problem of balancing and of course I was his dear friend. On the other hand, Thomas was competitive with either me or Kevin. Nevertheless, my husband simply did not care about me anymore. My husband used to tell me that I had the strength of three men put together. Maybe something else was on his mind. Kevin was always behind me and if I had a problem, he gave me his hand. Thomas and I fished many times in that area under the bridge. We went further up stream, past the bridge, and there was a huge hill. There was a white house at the top. The house was small but every time I went fishing, I had to stop at that place and look up. I thought to myself, *Someday, I would like to live in a place like this.* I knew it was my bubbly dream but I'd rather had a bubbly dream than none.

The summer of 1994 had been gone by quickly and I had time to take the citizenship test in Detroit. Kevin had helped me memorize some of the harder questions and I had been passing with him. I was all set to take the test. Thomas took me to the American Embassy

167

and I had no problem passing the test. For the first time I felt like I won the biggest trophy. On the way, Thomas called Kevin and gave him the fabulous news. I finally became an American Citizen on July 18, 1994 and the three of us went to the American Embassy. We had two plans: we would be going to Canada and then camping. We went to Canada and enjoyed the trip.

On our way from Canada, however, Kevin stopped at the Canadian Check Point. The officer questioned me about where I was from and asked for my passport. As I showed my passport to the officer I said that I was Korean and American. The officer told us to get out of the car and took us inside of a building. They searched our clothes and I had to show them what was in my purse. Then, the officers in the outside almost stripped the car. They did not find anything and we did not have any criminal records so they let us go quickly. We got into the car both of them asked me at the same time, "What was that all about?" I was Korean but I became an American citizen. The answer I'd given the answer the officer of two nationalities was because I just had gotten my American Citizenship, and I was proud of it. That day, both them had something to laugh about.

After that, we planned on going camping in Grayling, Michigan. I was so happy and I was flying above the clouds without knowing what would be waiting for me. I lived in the bubble without future plans because I'd paid such a price for my life, and I did not know how to fix it. Except I had experienced an unstoppable fire in me which I eventually discovered.

It was the first week of July 1994 and within a few days I would be inviting guests and Thomas' friends. I was making plans for my husband's birthday and he was turning 30. He hardly ever had a big party like this one and I wanted to make it special so that he would remember it the rest of his life. I told Kevin Thomas could not know anything and it was our secret. He gave me suggestions on what would be made for food, cake, drinks and so on. I had never met

Kevin's mom and dad so I also invited them, along with his brother. I started shopping for the birthday and I had to buy a lot because Thomas' family was a huge. I ordered special ribs and Kevin would be barbecuing. Also, he had to make a special drawing of a gun. Thomas loved to have a handgun and I let him have it even though I hated it. Kevin knew what the gun looked like because they visited the shooting range together. His drawing was done and I took it to the Dairy Queen. I ordered an ice cream cake, the biggest size they had.

I spent a lot of money for my husband's birthday. I felt that I may never see him again, whatever the reason. Above all, I'd made it through a very long journey with him. We had some great times but mostly in darkness. I was the one strong enough and made it through as far as I could go. His birthday came and everyone starting to arrive. Kevin came first because I told him to, and his folks and brother would come later. Kevin was cooking and I was setting up tables out in the yard. Thomas was surprised; he didn't expect a big birthday party. It took me a long time to learn what his family was like and I began accepting them. I knew this would be the first party and the last but no one knew, even Kevin.

All of Thomas' family was there and soon, Kevin's family arrived. Kevin introduced me to his parents and his mom brought something for me also. I took her into the kitchen and I opened it. It was a brass dolphin made of crystal. I'd received a priceless gift, worth more than a billion dollars. I thanked her and showed Thomas and Kevin later. Everyone was happy talking about our new house, how clean the place was. I kept things around home nice. I did not like anyone saying to me, "Korean, so and so …" Thomas did not like a dirty house because of how he grew up. The house was all Thomas' and he achieved it all by himself. I felt nothing for it. Kevin thought that our marriage was perfect because I never made a sound. I was crumbled, broken inside thousands of pieces but I kept a perfect cover for others.

Things between Kevin and me grew the day the three of us went to the embassy. Thomas had taken me there with his work clothes on, and Kevin met us there. We got to the swearing-in room, and Kevin started taking pictures of me. I'd stood with the Judge, next to the American flag. Thomas had kissed me and told Kevin to take me home and left. I was bummed out. I was looking forward to this day, that I would have something special to remember but I did not. At least, I had Kevin taking me home and that was good enough.

On the way home, I looked at Kevin's face. He was sad and unusually quiet that morning. I asked him, "What's the matter?" I knew he was pissed off. He was realizing what was happening with Thomas but Kevin could not say anything because it wasn't his problem and he had no right. On the other hand, I was stupid and a coward. I felt for Kevin a long time ago but I could not show my true feelings. It seemed to me that Kevin and I were meant to be on an eternal journey together. My head was pounding rapidly and I had to get out of the car. I told him to stop at the Big Boy restaurant, the corner where his house was. I had to slow down the way I was thinking.

We were sitting at the restaurant. I wanted him to say something but he was quiet. I ordered breakfast and he ordered a drink. He watched me. I did not want to look at him because I was afraid he would say something and I had no answer. He dropped me at my home. I was getting out of his car and said to him, "I will pick you up within a couple of hours." He drove away and I began cleaning my home. I had to be done within two hours, because both of us planned on going shopping at Meijer. I drove to his home and he was in the kitchen cleaning the stove. His stereo was playing Sade's "Bullet-Proof Soul." He asked me how I liked the song. I asked him replay it for me and he did. The more I heard the song, the more it caused sadness in my heart. He didn't know why he liked the song, and the next song played. We both liked "No Ordinary Love." The song had spoken to both of us deep in our souls, and as I listened, my heart trembled. I wanted to find some place to hide myself from him forever. At the grocery store, we bought things for the camping trip. As we passed each aisle, we held hands and sometimes, I held his arm and he let me. I was like a little girl hanging on to her daddy's arm and did not want to let go, and if she did she would lose him forever.

We forgot who we were at the moment and I wanted it to last. It was the first time I held his hand and I felt that I could hear his heartbeat. I saw a glimpse of what I thought it was like to be truly loved by someone. Kevin had been given me friendship and the opportunity to grow. He showed me how truly deep love could be. I had never felt like this before with my husband.

We returned from shopping. On the way to my house, I held his hand again. He told me we should not be holding hands. I told him not to worry about it. He helped me in with the groceries. I asked him to stay with me for a little while. I told him to sit on the couch. I put groceries in the refrigerator and I sat next to him. I hugged him and held him as hard as I could. I heard his heartbeat and his face blushed with innocence. Indeed, we were like little children because I never experienced what it was like being a child and Kevin, really was an innocent boy. He had a lot of experience with women but he had never seen a woman like me. As I climbed into his lap I held his hands tightly and leaned my head on his wide chest. I was scared and confused by my own actions toward Kevin. I rested my head for awhile, and he let me. I wanted him very much. If I didn't stop, what would happen to my marriage?

I was at a self-destructive point: the unstoppable passion, the burning fire which I controlled and held down for all sorts of reasons. I'd reached the point in my life of "no more nice girl" and I wanted to shave off my mask. *Did I want to trade this very moment for all those years of an empty, hollowed heart, a loveless marriage? Was I trying to find out what real love was through Kevin? Was this the reason I came to the United States?* I felt that Kevin started holding me tighter and tighter and he could not wait anymore. He kissed me passionately. It was sudden but we wanted each other for a very long time. Maybe we had to wait for seven years and it was finalizing our friendship. At this moment I could trace back to the first moment I encountered him on the sidewalk in Detroit at Thomas' old house. There was something that I felt when he looked at me.

Here we were. He said, "You want something from me." I said to him, "Sh-sh . . . nothing, just stay and hold me for a little longer, please." They were the longest minutes of my life ever. Both of us were afraid of a choice we were about to make but we could not stop. We could not control ourselves sexually and for me it was long overdue. The man I was married to hadn't satisfied me for seven years. Why? We finally had what we had been searching for and I took Kevin into my heart without any hesitation. We knew we could not look directly in each other's eyes. I understood what he was thinking and probably he also sensed that what my thought was. Both of us felt that guilt and confusion. Like a slow bullet that hit my broken, lonely soul and it penetrated the deepest part of being. We made love. I would love him through eternity. I knew I would. I realized what had happened. I knew what true love was once I took him into my heart and shared with respect. He gave me all who he was and I took every ounce of what he had. A special friendship grew deeper in my heart, more than I could handle. I wasted a friendship, and I was in agony. I knew I would be paying the price for it, but at the same time I was terrified of losing a priceless friendship. Kevin asked me if we could keep it our secret and I agreed.

He went home. My husband came home and he asked me to go to celebrate. I went along. I talked him about Kevin and I went to the grocery store and bought things for the camping trip. He began to talking about his work, but I had no interest. I wanted to see Kevin at that moment and wondered what he was doing, what he was thinking. In my heart there was something that I could never get rid of and it was like an imprint.

We came home and there was a message. Kevin wanted to visit us as soon as we came home. Thomas called him back, and soon Kevin knocked on our front door. I opened, and there he was. A huge grin was on his face and he handed me a box. He'd said, "This is for you." I opened the box. It was a half sheet cake decorated in the colors of the American flag with plastic balloons, and in the middle, the word "Congratulations." I thanked and hugged him as normal as possible. We had sat around for awhile, just talking. Kevin asked Thomas if he believed in God. Thomas' answer was that the Bible was just as any other book and all that was for moral purposes or based on human evolution. In their conversations, the subject had been changed about me. I did not remember all of it but Kevin said to my husband that I was searching for who I was. Kevin had figured it out by himself. He knew now that what did happen earlier and why it happened.

A few days went by and Kevin came to visit as usual. In his mind, nothing had happened. He recorded some of the music I liked to hear. Some of the singers I did not know, but I became used to the tunes. What he had recorded was something that he could read my heart, and through the songs I could hear what his heart wanted.

At one point I wanted survive in my marriage to Thomas. If I could just stay a little longer with my husband I would change. I wanted to and yet, I cared about him more, but it seemed to me we were drifting further away every day.

It was July 28, 1994; I waited for this day a long time. I was looking forward to going on a camping trip to Grayling. We set up the tent and went fishing in the river. The Manistee River was freezing cold even in the summer and we had to wear waders. It was going to be another great fishing day for us and we all would have lovely time. For a while, I wanted to forget about everything and enjoy fishing and breathe with nature. I needed time to make dinner with what we caught, and after dinner we would go walk. Kevin loved it very much. I could not tell what he was thinking but I was

173

glad that he was with us. I was sincere because I could hear his voice and his laughter.

After dinner, we all went walking along the Manistee River. The sun was setting; I took Kevin's picture. He posed behind the oldest pine tree and leaned his back on it. There was a wood fence standing along the riverbank. I took many pictures of him. He also photographed me and Thomas. I was acting like an innocent, sweet girl again. Kevin was closer to me again. I wanted to hold his hand as we walked but I had to control myself. I had to show my husband that I was happy and that I was having a wonderful time. As we were walking, I had to think about the approaching night, what would it be like and how was I going to control myself.

The night was falling deeper into dead silence. The only sound I heard was the running river. Both of them wanted to build the campfire so all three of us picked up the branches and The jet color of the sky and the full moon showed its face to the river, and the river glittered like a thousand shining diamonds. The campfire was burning; I lay down on the sandy ground and counted the stars as far as my eye could reach. Both of them were toasting the marshmallows and one of them asked me if I wanted to smoke. I did not know what that was. It was my first time experience with marijuana. Both of them knew what it felt like and they did not warn me. I had a couple of puffs and looked up at the sky. The pine trees were like some kind of humans watching me. I know I said something to them and I heard Kevin said that I was hallucinating.

Whatever I saw that night made me scared, but I had great memories. Thomas wanted to go to sleep. I was following my husband and said to Kevin, "Are you coming?" He said, "In a minute." We got into the tent. Thomas gave me a goodnight kiss and turned over on the other side. I could not close my eyes. I thought I was wasted but I could not fall asleep. Kevin returned to the tent. He lay down quietly. He thought I was sleeping but I waited for him to return. Suddenly, I remembered when I met my Korean ex-boyfriend on my first fishing trip. Thomas, Kevin, and I lay in the tent and I was in the middle. It was daizaboo. The only difference between the past and now was that it was two men instead two women. Kevin and I secretly held hands and fell asleep.

Sixteen

The next morning, Thomas woke up very early and he did not want to miss the morning fishing because usually fish feeding time was about sunrise. Kevin and I were alone again. We decided to take a walk along the riverbank before Thomas' return. Then, we would have breakfast and we would be going upstream. We held hands as we walked without talking. Suddenly, we stopped and turned to one another. We kissed passionately. He held me and rubbed my back like a little child. I could let my being flow with him forever. We were like a burning fire and he gave me sexual satisfaction for the first time in my life. I wanted him more and more. It was like a magnet. With Kevin, I had intimacy, a wild ride, passion and the most wonderful sex ever. I asked Kevin to carry me on his back. He carried me like my dad did for me when I was a little girl.

I did not need money. I did not want to have things. I just wanted to have someone who would show me his heart. Was I dangerous? Yes, I was dangerous. Did I love Kevin? Yes, I did. Was I needy? Yes, I was hungry for someone to care for me. Kevin was a sweet man and the way he treated me wouldn't last but I had to give all I could so that I could find myself.

We came for breakfast. Thomas came back from fishing and waited for us to return. He asked me where we were. I told him downstream. We had breakfast and left for the Au Sable River. We rented a rowboat and we were going for rainbow trout. Thomas and Kevin were rowing the boat. I was in the middle and scared because I could not see the bottom of the river. Both of them had no experience rowing the boat but I trusted them. They not were going to drown me in the cold water. I was talking to them, and they thought that it was funny. I saw them giggling like children.

On the ride back, I sat in the back of the car with Kevin up front. No one could hear my cry. The storm was rising in my heart and my heart was hurting like a piece had been cut out from the heart. I know my precious friendship with the gentle man and only lover, he would be slipping away but how could I protect myself and Kevin? We dropped Kevin at his home and we came back to our home but Thomas had to leave for work. His partners had called to say that they had an emergency part to deliver. I called Kevin and asked him to come over. We made love once more. Kevin told me he could not do this anymore. I agreed, and he left. It was August 2, 1994, the anniversary of the day I cremated my mother in 1982.

The scorching summer heat changed to an icy cold winter on my back. Kevin had been holding my back and he had been my shadow for the most human basic need, emotional support. He was in my heart but that wasn't enough. I wanted to see him, touch him and hear his voice. He gave me everything that he had, and in return, I had given him my heart. I trusted him and asked him to stay a little longer but he couldn't. I tried finding my way out from this world forever and it got harder. My broken spirit began to despair and each day was fading away. I would not rise above it because there was no strength and the guilt had eaten away at me little by little. I had nothing else to give or receive. I was struggling once more with life and faced destruction. The only solution I had was to disappear from this world. I was living in the place of purgatory and it trapped me forever. I promised Kevin that whatever happened between us, the secret would forever stay in my heart and I meant to keep it.

On August 10, 1994 the day was ugly, dreary, rainy. Once more, tragedy struck my life. I did kill myself three times already and I did not go, but this time I knew I would go. I wanted to hear Kevin's voice while I was alive. I called him and he came. I told him that I could not go on with this marriage, and I had no reason to try. He held me and said I should go to work to be around other people and not be isolated.

I did not agree. I told Kevin that I was going to work but instead of going to work, I went to the drugstore. I bought 60-70 sleeping pills. I saw that Kevin had been following me. I lost him. He knew something was up but he had never thought that I would really act on it. I came home and took most of the pills with whiskey. I waited five or ten minutes for the pills to start liquefying, and I called Kevin again. He asked me, "Where are you?" I told him I was home, but I would have to leave home because of my guilt. I could not face my husband, and I lost my dear friend and lover. In this world, I'd said, there was no place that I could stay and be happy. It was the right thing to do and I was happy to go home. I told him, "I love you."

I was about to hang up the phone when I saw a police car and an ambulance parked in front of my house. I told him, "I hate you." I hung up the phone. I tried to get out of the house and my husband came home and he stopped me. I told him I wanted go to see my mom. Where there was water, my mom would be there. While I was talking to Thomas, I saw Kevin's white Thunderbird parked across the street. Everyone tried to get me into the ambulance but I fiercely refused. I would rather die on the ground than go to a crazy hospital. I walked out the door. I knew I was dizzy from the pills and my eyesight was fading, but I could see Kevin's face. He was standing by the car and he didn't know what to do to help me. The pills affected me greatly. I fell down in the ditch, but I had the strength to get up and walk toward Kevin's car. He watched me, not saying anything. I held onto his car and said to him, "I hate you." I told him I would not go in the ambulance. I fell once more and I think he grabbed me. I may remember but I was not really sure. Kevin may have taken me to the hospital because I remember someone putting my legs into the car, and I woke up in the hospital.

I do not know how long I was in the hospital. When I woke up, I was tied to the four corners of the bed. My husband said to me, "Hi, Carol." I saw Thomas' face and it was pock-marked with dark color, like when I was a teenager, when the man tried to rape me in that motel room. I said to him something and someone said that I was having a hallucination. A few days later I came home and told Thomas that I would be a good wife. I begged him not to send me to the crazy hospital. Thomas told me that I had refused go to the hospital. The only way I agreed to go was with Kevin.

I promised to see a psychiatrist for my illness. Thomas made an appointment for twice a week. My therapist wasn't a "doctor." She was really calm and knew how to listen. I told her what I could not tell anyone, especially my husband, for almost two years. I told her about Kevin and how much he was meant for me, and what kind of love I have in my heart. Somehow, I was blamed for the entire thing that happened to us. Somehow I was the one pushed to the edge of no return. I had walked through the darkness alone and I did not know how to get out of it. Kevin gave me what I needed the most when I needed it but how could he turn away like nothing had happened? I did not understand.

The therapist listened quietly, then gave me her peace of mind. Through her I did understand the feelings toward Kevin. It wasn't just the marriage but also there were too many wounds of the past which I had never dealt with before. I had a better feeling about Kevin and I thought about who I was. I had unbreakable strength but I was also building a wall inside that was immeasurably thick and no one could get through to me. My husband, on other hand, was just a simple guy and I was looking for more than he could give me. This was the beginning of my true understanding of love.

I told the therapist about my childhood, which was unknown to my husband's family. I was getting my strength back as quickly as possible but also the doctor prescribed Prozac. The dangerous time had passed. I returned to work and I truly wanted to be a good wife.

I wanted to go back to the way it was, to the innocence we had in Korea. We had been changing over time but if we really loved each other we could go back. I did a lot of thinking about the direction for our lives together. Thomas promised me he would be with me and that was the reason he bought a home for us. He did not tell me this before. Thomas had problems, too. He never discussed anything that truly mattered in marriage and we did not share our intimacy with openness. I wanted to know how I could make it better.

The therapist told me to always come back to see her until I could get a grip on my life. What had happened in my life, I couldn't go back to fix. Therefore, the only thing I could do was to push forward. It was the therapist's advice and I took it. I was really getting better and happier and then, Kevin showed up. The three of us went bowling once more. He asked me how I was doing. When I saw Kevin, I was crumbling again because of my shame and guilt. He did really well by me but I betrayed him for no reason. I caused too many people to get hurt, whether consciously or unconsciously. I was being eaten away by a thousand questions in my head. I did not hate this man, and I still really loved Kevin. I did not say much to him while we were bowling but I had unfinished businesses with him. I thought my time would come and someday I would ask and I wanted to hear his answer honestly.

A month and a half passed the last time I saw Kevin. When I was on the road, we still passed each other in many places. Before the holiday season, I called Kevin. I asked him why I was the one pushed to the edge, and what made him become cold as ice. What was the reason he did what he did? He told me that I did not deserve anything. I knew he was blaming me for the suicide attempt and he said I did it while in Korea but why in the United States? I had a husband and I had a good friend. He forgot what he had done to me and he said everything was my fault. He did not see himself for who he was. He was a monster cowering under a thick mask and he did not want to see the truth. He said that I did not deserve anything, and they were the most hurtful words I had heard from anyone. I just took them and buried them deep in my heart. I did not know how to express my feelings and of course, I still didn't speak English well. Kevin came by again around the holidays. I was uneasy but I kept it under control. I called him a few more times and asked him to forgive me and be my friend again.

About a week before Christmas, Thomas returned from work. I told him what had happened with Kevin during the summer, and what caused me to try and take my own life. I was telling him the truth. I did not want to live my life in darkness anymore. I knew I was paying the price, but it was the only way out; if I could clean my heart, we could start again. Thomas listened quietly but he had no reaction. Actually, he said to me that I was better than Kevin. I thought about what he meant. He was thanking me for telling him the truth, but there were other things on his mind that I had no way to detect. Maybe something had been on his mind for a very long time, waiting to happen.

The next morning, Thomas visited Kevin. When Thomas returned, he said he would get even with me and left. Thomas started going out every night. He had wanted to go out chasing other women but had waited for a long time. I heard the truth from him. He told me that I did not trust him. He did everything he could but he did not know how to please me. He wanted to have a passionate relationship with me but I did not agree. I realized we had too many problems in ourselves but both of us did not want to admit it. Then Kevin came into our lives so that we both could see what each other was missing. I was not mad at Kevin anymore because of the truth about Thomas.

Maybe Kevin was the one used by both of us. On the other hand, Kevin had taken me out of a dead marriage. Suddenly, I awoke from my sleep. My marriage ended quickly, and so did my friendship with Kevin.

I do not remember how I spent my birthday and Christmas that year. I never got to celebrate my birthday like Thomas did. He never gave me a surprise party and the only thing he did was take me out to dinner. He never gave me anything special except for the one time he brought flowers from the street corner when he came back from National Guard field training. In the totality of our marriage years, I only had great sex once.

I hated this holiday. Thomas went out and I stayed home. He was getting even with me, exactly what he promised. He slept someplace else and came home in the morning. He just couldn't get rid of me. He had no idea who I was and why I lived the way I lived. I did not choose to live that kind of life, and it had hurt me enormously. I let him do whatever he had to do to get his anger out and if he still had love for me someday he would stop. I still had hope. I waited for him because I was remembering the things we said to each other a long time ago: we would try at least three times if we had problems in our marriage.

Nevertheless, I hoped to get better but it was my bubbly dream. I did not see it was coming and I did not prepare for it. It was in innocence that I still hoped for Thomas to return. It was January 3rd 1995. Thomas returned from work. As he was taking off his boots he said, "You will be getting a paper from someone." His voice was firm but calm. I asked him, "What kind of paper?" I still did not understand what he was talking about, the "paper." He told me I would be getting some papers from his lawyer. For a few minutes I could not talk or breathe. The entire universe was falling down on me and my body became numb. I did not feel anything and the ticking bomb I had carried for so long was ready to go off. I took a deep breath. I was pretending in a loveless marriage and went through all those years without complaint because it was the right thing for me to do. When I took a deep breath, I felt myself sinking into the black hole. I did not have tears and I did not have a reaction when I really needed them. I stood in the kitchen holding a spatula;

I had been cooking our dinner.

I couldn't think of anything except where I might be tomorrow. That was my only thought. I sensed that my legs were shaking and anger grew inside of me. I was tired. I had to sit down in the kitchen chair for a few minutes to calm myself. Thomas came to sit down next to me, and tried to explain to me. Suddenly, I got up from my chair and pushed him to the end of the kitchen. I knew he was a cold-hearted person, sending me divorce papers without my knowledge; it was as cold as it could get. At least Kevin had regrets because he knew he contributed to the way I was. Thomas was something else. I lived with him as if I didn't exist. When I talked to him, I talked to a wall. He had lied. He had made up his mind a long time ago. Everything that he wanted in his life he got; his career, success financial stability. In addition, he had a home and business. What did I get from him? I did not get anything except a broken heart from two men.

How could I adjust for myself? I was walking in the shadow of darkness and no one could bring me out to the sun. I wished that there was an ending in my life because I had been fighting for 37 years and truly wanted to stop. I was just getting over the first attempt in August, and here I was thinking about it again five months later.

I shoved Thomas in the kitchen and ran out. I was still not a good driver, but I planned on going out somewhere in Ann Arbor. It was winter and the road was slippery. In my thoughts, it was a great plan and if it worked I knew at least someone would recognize my name from my license; at least, someone could take care of my body after the "accident." I was still ahead and better than I used to live in Korea. If it worked, it would be a perfect car accident on a winter road and no one would ever know. Thomas would not say anything and Kevin would have to deal with it the rest of his life. I hoped that it would work. I drank while I drove. I took Warren Road and passed Venoy where Kevin's house was. Then, I turned left to Ford Road. I was almost to M-14 and within 50 feet I would be on the freeway.

Without reason, my car turned itself around and stopped. Why? I have no other recollection of that day. My car had stopped, then turned to the east. The engine was still running. I held the steering wheel and cried. I was talking to myself, to the empty air. *What did I do wrong? Why was my life so hard?* I wanted to die but I could not do that either. All my life, I never lived with anything; no money, success or love and I never complained. I had a simple small dream most women want, a home with a loving husband. I lived my life without hurting anyone. *What else could I do? What else should I do? Where do I go from here?* I went through life and death many times and came through all sorts of hardships that other people could not even imagine. I was the person at 37 who had tasted the sweet and bitter of life. The only thing I wanted was love that was simple, honest and sincere. *Was that too much to ask?* I was devastated. I had a stream of questions but there were no answers. My tears stopped and I could drive. The only place I could go was to my home. I was still the wife of Thomas and maybe I could try again. I knew I wasn't a quitter. Something was trapped inside of me and it was screaming to get out.

I was calm and I could drive. When I was out of my house I was angry and could not think or see things clearly, but it had changed within a few hours. I did not know what made the fire go out so quickly and only the thing in my head was maybe . . . I was still driving and looked at the clock. It was after midnight and getting toward one o'clock. It was dead quiet on the street. I came to Ford Road and Venoy, a few blocks south of Kevin's house.

I saw all streetlights were dim and yellowish, but there was one really bright light standing out in the mist of the winter night. I turned around my car and absent-mindedly followed the light to the building. I knocked but the door was open. A lady had heard the knock; she came to the door and held it open for me to come in. She was wearing a white gown and the first thing she said was, "You needed to cry." I held her and cried for a while. She said, "Come.

My pastor is in the back. I will tell him you are here. What is your name?" I told her, "Kay." She left me on a chair in the waiting room and left. I did not see anything in that building I recognized.

I waited for a few minutes and in walked an elderly man. He had white hair and was very tall. He said, "I am Pastor so and so." I could not register in my head what a pastor was. He said to come into the office. I followed him in and I saw the Bible. I realized that I was in a church but I did not know exactly what a church was. He explained that he was a pastor who worked at night. He had lost his beloved wife and since then he usually worked late. He asked me, "How could I help you?" I told him very briefly what was going on in my marriage. The first words he said were, "If your husband really loves you, you shouldn't get divorced." He explained further that no matter how difficult a relationship was, I shouldn't get divorced and we should work through it together. He was like the woman therapist I met in August, about five months before.

The pastor gave me a piece of paper and told me: "On this paper, you need to write." He had a paper folded in half and told me to write on one side about the good things both of us did while we were married and on the other half, what we did wrong. It was a long nine years of marriage because a woman still did not know how to talk.

I thanked him and went home. It was 2:00 in the morning, and I thought about it for a moment. Through his wisdom, I found encouragement and strength, but I decided on the divorce. I had lacked experience with people all my life and because of it my life was really difficult. My tears had stopped and I realized my heart and brain were working together. I had sudden courage and my brain told me that I would go on with my life once more and I would try harder. Through the pastor, I gained much more than any other person had given to me and I was suddenly eager to live. I wanted to show the world that I would not give up my life for worthless men. There was a bitter taste of anger in my mouth at the two men in my life and maybe the whole world of men.

The next morning I told Thomas I was ready for divorce papers and I went to work. When I got to work, I asked some co-workers about my situation. They knew I was in the hospital a few months ago; however, they appreciated what my husband had done because after all, he took me back. They thought that Thomas was a great man and a saint but when they heard the truth from me about what was going on in my life, they thought twice about my husband. They knew I did my duty without knowing much about life in the United States.

My co-worker told me that in the United States no one divorced without a lawyer. I had no idea what the law was in the United States. Then I told them about what had happened with Kevin too. They all had something to say about him as well. I was a naive person—new to everything— without friends who truly cared about me. One of the co-workers gave me a lawyer's phone number and she said, "I called him and you will be going to meet him in this office." I told her thanks, but she added, "When you go home do not say anything until you meet the lawyer." I went home and I did not say anything. I still did not feel anything. I felt hollow. I was not hungry nor could I think straight. I just waited for the sun to rise in the morning. Every moment at a time, I had different views about my life. Some moments, I didn't think I would make it through the night but in other moments, I had so much strength I could go on forever.

Seventeen

A few days later, I went back to the church on Sunday. I was
awaiting in the hallway for the Sunday morning service. I looked
around the hallway, the walls, and the ceiling of the church. I had
gazed at the paintings on the wall. I did not know who Jesus was,
I just saw a man holding onto the children in his arms. Actually, I
went to church when my husband and I were in Korea but I really
did not pay attention. In other words, I had no recollection of seeing
this man on the painting before. While I was looking around in the
hallway, many children were running around wildly. I thought the
church had restrictions about misbehaving, but this church was
different. The Pastor saw me and called someone to take me into the
service and she asked me to sit next to her. I did not know how to
follow the rhythm but I remembered the song. After the service, the
Pastor asked me to visit again and encouraged me to come to Bible
class also. I'd told him, "I will try."

I was in the middle of a mess in my life, and in the meantime
I had to make it to work. I did not have any money to spare with
a place like church, or the time. I was worried about the most
important thing in my life: surviving in the United States. I also told
Thomas about the church, how I felt about going to the church. He'd
said that might be just what I needed. I felt better getting out of the
relationship.

I was still living in my home in Garden City until my lawyer told
me exactly what to do, but also I was just mad at Thomas because

Thomas already had a teenage girlfriend with a baby from someone else. He liked her very much and brought her into the house. I accepted my situation was and I just broke into tears when he wasn't around. I was furious. I was a noble wife to him through the end of our marriage but he did not respect me as a human. I had fear of him sending me back to Korea and because of it I kept my mouth shut. I knew he had plan but I never sensed his devious, calculating side to his personality and I just wanted to get out of there as soon as I could, but everything had its own time. I had great patience all my life and I would wait a little longer. He was still my husband and we'd shared things together, so I made myself as calm as I could.

Then one day Thomas told me that I left my heart on the ground so that Kevin and he could step all over it. I was hurt. I did not say anything. I yielded because of what the circumstances were, but someone who knew how to hurt me like that would face justice. What Thomas and Kevin said to me was indescribable. I know it wasn't me who hurt them. Yes, I made a mistake, but both of them knew what was going on. Both of them let it happen because I gave many messages that I was hurting and I was lonely. I came from a different culture and did not know the language, plus, I did not have much education. I was an easy target to many American people, but I did not know how to stand up for myself.

In February of 1995, I received divorce papers from Thomas' lawyer. It stated what he wanted and what he was willing to divide. He would give me the Bronco II and the jewelry he bought which was part of the settlement. I would also get $500 a month for two years. He would keep his business for himself. I almost said yes because I'd felt that what I did was guilty and I did not have any right. I thought he'd given me something at least, and I was thankful but I took the paperwork with me. My co-worker called the lawyer and he looked at the papers. My lawyer said, he would be talking to Thomas and I would be out of the picture for awhile until he got what I was entitled to. The lawyer told me that I could not survive on $500 a month.

My boss looked at the papers and she was angry, too. In America, gifts and presents were not part of settlements, and it should be 50/50 no matter what. Also, I was getting divorced, but he had contributed to it so therefore, I should not be guilty about a thing. My lawyer told me he would negotiate with Thomas' lawyer. Thomas thought that I would never figure things out and he tried to manipulate things until the end of the divorce. My lawyer asked the other party about the financial statement and other statements. Thomas came up with a proposal and that if I paid my share of the lawyer fees, he would pay me $1,000 a month for three years. It was a fair settlement and Thomas and I finally agreed. It was a very small amount compared to the way I lived for nine years of our marriage. I thought about at least, I was in the United States and I became an American Citizen and therefore, no money could replace my heart. Above all, I helped him to build for the future and his life was all set. It was going to take some time to get where I wanted to be but I would survive no matter what. We did not have an ugly battle getting divorced because I had a mild demeanor and Thomas did also. I was not a greedy person and I never was. As far as I was concerned with money, it was just paper; I looked at a diamond ring as a rock.

We were still waiting for our paperwork to be finalized, and in the meantime, we went to dinner together and Thomas found me an apartment. I found a one bedroom apartment in Southfield, Michigan. It had a kitchen, living room and was spacious; I thought I would make to the top, starting from this place. I was unfamiliar with everything in life but I knew how to survive. I had survived before and I would do so again. Thomas took me to my new apartment and helped me sign the lease. I had to wait for a month, however, because a tenant would be move out by the end of March. We were still living together and we were coming home after the signed lease. On the way I had tears. He said to me, "You will be alright. Your strength is three men put together." In my mind, I said, *Thanks a lot.*

That was the reason you did not care about me? I could not believe what he'd just said. He was the wall that I never got through.

The only reason I was still living with him was because he did not want me to be homeless. I was homeless until I met Thomas. I did not live on the street but in one place after another. I just knew I did not belong to the Earth but I wasn't sure why I felt that way all my life. I was only thirty-eight years old but it seemed to me I had been living over a thousand years all alone. Every day I had to deal with car problems and Thomas did not care anymore but people who worked with me were the greatest. They gave me some places to go to check my car and there was a man waiting for me. I knew I had to get out of Thomas' house. I could have stayed a little longer and Thomas told me to but if I did, I would have had a heart attack. I just couldn't breathe, and I was suffocating when I saw Thomas. So after the man fixed my car, I asked him to help me move my sewing machine. He would bring his truck to Garden City, and I had to bring out my sewing machine to his truck. I did not have any place to go in the world.

The only solution I had was finding a cheap motel for a month. I found one on Eight Mile Road and Telegraph, the Blue Bird Motel. It was close to work and I would be much happier than stay at Thomas'. People called this area really bad but I did not care. The motel charged $30 a day but for me little less because I was going to be there only a month and the motel gave me a discount. I did not have cash but I had a credit card with a $11,000 line of credit. It had arrived just before I was getting divorced and it helped me in many ways. My bitterness was rising and there was no way I could stop thinking about all sorts of things eaten away inside me. My hardship-filled life began again. I packed some of my clothes and the machine. I was sewing lab coat patches for the promotional company after work in the office, and by evening, I did work at the motel cleaning in Roseville, Michigan.

Finally, on April 5, 1995 my apartment was ready to move in

to, and also, I signed my divorce papers the same day. I did not go to court because I did not speak English well and therefore, my lawyer took care of all the paperwork. The only problem I had in my mind was, *How will I pay for this apartment?* If I could not make the payments, I would be homeless. I had no idea how much living there would cost. When I signed the divorce papers, the lawyer told me I would make it. He encouraged me and so did my co-workers. I began cleaning motels at night for a few nights a week. I had worked as a maid when I was young and I thought I would never do this kind of work again, ever. However, I had to. I had fear about working in motels, especially cleaning, because I saw some awful things. I promised that I would never let myself work in a motel or club where there were men doing things when the night fell. For a while, I cried a lot every night. My tears wouldn't stop but I had to work much harder than before. I tried to forget as fast as I could but something held me tight.

A few months passed living in my apartment. I began to find all sorts of stores around the area. A couple of miles up was Greenfield, where my lawyer was, and from my apartment on West 11 mile was Southfield Road. One Sunday morning, I was driving around I discovered a small Lutheran Church. When I opened the door, it was the middle of the Sunday service that was being led by a teenager. She was reading a scripture and I thought it was strange. I didn't have the experience of youth in church programs and in truth I didn't know why the teenager was reading the Bible. I did not care for the service and I thought I would search for another church. I was sitting farther back by the door while people were sharing peace.

After the service, I was about to leave when a woman introduced herself. She was so and so and right away we went to lunch together at a Greek restaurant nearby. I talked about my life and explained that I was still going through a grieving period. Then, we met again at the church. We then met every week in the church. We became friends and by May and June, my life was getting a little easier for me emotionally. I was used to being alone but feared loneliness. I decided to talk to the pastor. He had been seeing me in the church every week. I never missed one service up to that point. I visited the pastor ad briefly talked with him about what was happening, how I was still living in my husband's shadow. He told me he was married, divorced and got remarried. Since his remarriage, he had been happy with himself and the second marriage was better than the first one. His advice was to keep working hard, go to church, and pray. He said he would like to see what God had planned for me. I realized that I had the strong ability to accomplish any goal with God on my side. However, I didn't really know who He was.

I kept thinking about Kevin. I'd waited for him to change his mind about me and come to see me. He was still with me, and when I closed my eyes, I could see, touch, and imagine he was taking to me all the time. I had a burning desire for the flame, the way he opened the deep unknown and I wanted to feel that again. I knew he did something to me no one else ever could. It was a wonderful experience I had with him, and I did not want to freeze my whole being. I had been sending many letters asking for his forgiveness and apology, and if there was anything that he could remember about us. I received no response from Kevin.

Whatever the reason, I couldn't shake him off completely. In my heart, there was a stone that I couldn't digest or couldn't dissolve, all I could do was just pray. I thought I was doing everything I could at the promotional company. The office manager and I had a disagreement, which made me really angry. It could had been prevented if I'd thought carefully before I spoke, but I did not have that kind of wisdom. Somehow, I was out of control. The years of hardship which had built inside of me finally got turned into an unstoppable rage, and I could not stay with people who told me what to do. I wanted to be free and this was the most significant way of finding out who I was.

I had to quit working the week of Thanksgiving in 1995. My boss, who was my manager's brother, told me, "Don't burn the bridge." I did not what that meant but he told me to visit them often and I knew I had built a good relationship with them. I talked to my friend from church about it. She said, sometimes there will be conflict with people I work with. It was not unusual and I needed to just accept it and move on. I did not remember what made me so angry.

The day was set for me to quit, and I did not know how to look for a job. The company owner asked one of the sales ladies if she knew anyone. The sales lady told me she would find out if someone she knew anyone was hiring. The next day she came to work and gave me a phone number for me for a cleaning job. She told me to call him after Thanksgiving. I had a few weeks' time off. I was okay with it because I needed time off somehow and I had a credit card to buy groceries. Also my boss gave me a holiday bonus check plus my two weeks' paycheck in his generosity. Moreover, Thomas had started paying me alimony so I was alright for awhile.

My friend suggested I should go home with her for the holidays in Illinois to her parents' place. I agreed. I packed up and took my brand new blue Jeep. I was happy. It was different because I had not seen any other state besides Louisiana. It was a long drive. I met my friend's parents and they reminded me of Thomas' parents. Their faces were lit up like the sun and I was their daughter. Her dad took me out on the farm and I rode a tractor the next morning, and I met most of her family. My friend had a huge family and they all got along well, just like Thomas' family.

The second night I dreamed about Thomas and Kevin. I thought that it was strange. I had a gut feeling I would be seeing Kevin very soon. It was just like how my mother always came to me to warn me about something before actual events took place. So I woke up and told my friend about it. She thought that it just a dream but I said to her it wasn't just a dream.

I had a well-spent first holiday with my friend. I enjoyed her company and her family. Maybe she was God-sent for me. The day we were to return to Michigan, we had breakfast with her parents, where I thanked them for their hospitality. I came home and dropped my friend on my way. When I got into the parking lot, I saw a Thunderbird backing up and turning the corner of the apartment complex. I thought it was strange and I felt that that car reminded me of Kevin's. It was the day after Thanksgiving, 26, 1995. I saw the Thunderbird leaving and I came in to my door. About five minutes later my phone rang. I picked up. He said, "Guess who?" I said, "Kevin!" I was terrified but also so happy I screamed. I told him, "You were just here." I explained him what I'd seen minutes before. He said that he was in a party store, and did I want anything to drink? I told him to get wine and an opener. I did not drink anymore, since that horrifying day.

He came in and looked around my apartment. He saw several of my paintings. He had a special interest in the painting of him on the camping trip, which I'd painted exactly from the photo. Then, he looked around little more on the wall and saw his drawing of Thomas with his signature on it, something I looked at every day. I imagined how he was like while he was working with that piece; I had a sentimental attachment to it for that reason. He said, "You are painting. Keep it up." I was just a beginner and I still had a long way to go to be perfect, but it was the only hobby that made me complete.

Kevin and I were shared a glass of wine and I was happy to see him again. As always, he was quiet and his face was blushed. He may have had a glass of something before he came to see me. He could not stop touching me while we were sitting next to each other. I knew I had been waiting for him for a long time. I hadn't let any man touch me since my divorce.

I made love to Kevin again. I did not know how it would affect my emotions but I did not think about emotional consequences. He did not say goodbye and left that night about after midnight. I saw the first snow was coming down pretty good. I told him, "Be careful driving."

I hadn't seen him for a while and I returned to work after Thanksgiving. I was still working at the motel and I did not like it (but what else I could find?) so I worked until the following spring. Meanwhile, I changed my career direction for cleaning and I became self-employed. In early December of 1995 I was my own boss and I had to organize my business for cleaning, and I felt that it would be a prosperous business. I called Kevin right away and told him what I would be doing. I asked Kevin to draw a logo for me. My company name was "Kay's Helping Hands," and the logo had something to do with hands. A couple of weeks later I met him in the restaurant on Telegraph Road. I didn't like the first drawing because it had too soft a woman's hand. I told him to draw it again. I wanted an image of ruggedness and the firmness of my hand holding a brush. He brought a second drawing and I loved it.

I was all set for starting my business. I told my interior design customer that if he gave me more clients I would not raise the price and I would charge $15 an hour. He agreed. He was a businessman and he owned an interior design company for a long time in Rochester. He was a good man and his family treated me like a friend. I was happy with my life, and living well doing cleaning. I quit the motel job, and as I quit, he found more clients for me. Within a month, I had eight to ten clients and they were really nice to me. I spent all day cleaning, and in the evenings, I took a painting class twice a week in Birmingham, Michigan.

I remained at my Lutheran church and became better at reading the Scriptures and understanding the sermons on Sunday service. Also, I took an oil painting class and I was busy all the time. All my life there had been no recreation available for me and it was fantastic to see myself doing something with an unfamiliar subject. Everything was going smoothly. I had filled my empty apartment with furniture from the credit card, and when my room was filled, I began to put all my energy into the blank, white stretched canvas. I captured my beautiful and innocent imagination with brushes and let the colors of the rainbow flow from my heart. Canvas became my wonderful, kind friend and filled my empty, lonely heart. One canvas after another started making me a happier person. I repainted Kevin's face, and the places we walked, talked, laughed and sat. I was beginning to discover just who I was. My eyes were burning tired but I could not drop the painting brush until 3:00-4.00 a.m. I had a passion for everything what I did. I had always admired artists, whether painters or writers. Anyone who had an artistic ability was to be admired. I was just like a kid in a candy store, like a child learning to talk and gain independence by walking. I absorbed information and knowledge from anything that I read. I read the picture on the wall while I cleaned a home. There was a poem, "Wing" by William Blake and that was the first piece I had ever read, but also, when I went to the Sunday service I would gain more knowledge by just listening.

Anything I saw or read, I soaked it up like a sponge. Some days moved dreadfully slow. Other days were filled with sadness and tears. I endured the pain all that I could, and kept moving forward with tears. I told my other self, "Kay you can do whatever comes your way."

Eighteen

The interior designer company owner gave me a raise. His business was doing well in Rochester Hills. My work had been highly praised, so he gave me more clients. He knew what made me happy. I was traveling at least 80 miles per day, and some days, I had two clients a day and I was exhausted and my body was burned out. Mentally, I still could not get over Kevin.

Finally, the magnificently colored autumn leaves were falling and the air was getting chilly. I had a plan for my first birthday party ever, with all my friends from church and art class. This was the first celebration of my birthday knowing God but I had been going to church less than a year. I invited the pastor and his wife. I bought everything and I made a Korean dish which everyone loved. I didn't have to buy my birthday cake because one of my friends made it for me. It was the greatest party ever. I'd lived life without any important celebrations but I could make myself my own birthday. It was something that I wanted to remember forever. It was the end of a quiet 1995 and I didn't know what kind of surprise was around the corner, but soon a good life would begin.

I was still struggling every day. I missed Kevin very much. I was obsessed with his tone of voice and my emotions were a wreck. I wished that I could hear from him once more. On top of emotional turmoil, I was using physical labor. For all my life I used all my strength and I'd decided to do a cleaning business again. It was financially somewhat lifting my burden but I was thinking myself, *Why did I choose this kind of business?* I did not have the answer. I hated the cleaning jobs so much, but something had to make sense in order to understand who I was. I had to clean houses every day, and some houses were unspeakably nasty. I was overwhelmed. I wasn't just cleaning; I volunteered to do the laundries and cooking. I thought that it was the only way I knew how to make clients happy. I was overworked and underpaid. I did not know why I had to impress people. I was doing almost everything in the house except, I wasn't anyone's wife.

The pastor of my church called me and said that he decided to baptize me as a God's child. He set the date for January 14, 1996. The pastor baptized me before the Sunday service began. I had a few girlfriends who came to church a little early and they witnessed I was God's child. The pastor read to me the baptismal creed and I followed. I was incredibly happy after the baptismal. I felt that something happened but I did not know what was happened. I was overjoyed. Everything I saw and touched had a different sense. I was like a crazy woman or like a child. It was first time in my life nothing bothered me. I laughed a lot and the cleaning job did not bother me anymore. I felt that I could fly without wings. I did not get hungry without eating all day. When I went to work for my Rochester client, they did not understand what I was feeling even though they were Christians. This client had two children and I was friendly with their son, who was easy to talk to.

After the baptismal there were mores questions. I was starting to think about why I came to work in Rochester and suddenly I remembered where I used to spend fishing trips with Thomas and Kevin; it was in Paint Creek in downtown Rochester. Once upon a time, we had sat under the beautiful branches of the trees and listened to the flowing stream of the creek. Was there some kind of connection to all this? The mysterious search had begun through every night and my thoughts and memories were rushing in like the tide in the ocean. I was hoping that Kevin would hold my hand and show me the way across to where I was headed. My questions remained unanswered and I started recalling my past through dreams, little by little, as soon as my head hit the pillow.

In the meantime, I invited Thomas and his girlfriend over to my apartment. Since the separation, Thomas had a few women but it seemed to me this one was real. I had no feeling of guilt or shame. I was comfortable with who I was. When I saw the both of them together, I realized that I was a nice, loving, kind person who had a big lion heart. I didn't build the wall between us even though it was hard a marriage. We had a nice dinner together and laughed and joked about something. I hoped that I showed them kindness and sincerity. At least, I wanted to save our friendship; we weren't a happy couple but more than likely a friendship might continue. I was busy working and got the feeling that nothing would worry me anymore. I decided to continue to go to church and really get some knowledge. In the middle of the night I woke up to write down all my dreams, and I went back to sleep. There was non-stop dreaming every night. Strangely, I remembered every detail, color, and place. Sometimes, I saw Kevin and Thomas together but they were very different people. They were human in reality but in my dream they were not. I just wrote details as best way I could.

One day I was cleaning and I saw a short poem: "No bird soars too high if he soars with his own wings" (William Blake). It was odd because I understood what it meant. He was talking about human strength. Humans must have more than basic senses. I had to look beyond human form because the rest of nature always relies on something in order to survive. I did not know what faith was, but I was guessed this had something to do with faith. My brain had not known how to slow down thinking or shut down. It was an exhausting battle but every day I was happy.

Then, Thomas called me on Memorial Day weekend and asked me to come join with his family, so I went. Everyone was swimming in the pool and I did not know how to swim. I sat with his sister and told her about what was going on in my life when I went to sleep. Thomas' sister told me that I had had a spiritual experience and it could be really good. I took her advice and kept it quiet for awhile. I had been baptized exactly five months June 15, 1996. I had been having dreams for a long time but this dream was different than others. I had an unrealistic, vividly colorful experience and it was a personal revelation. The highest power of spiritual existence, an existence of the non-practical world. The world that cannot be touched but it is here everywhere on earth, if people wanted to see it and yet, cannot be explained by my senses. It is as closed as any tree in my backyard, and maybe my neighbors. It is close as in our heart. Since then, it has touched me, changed me forever and it has been taking me on an unknown journey. As I am on the journey, my heart is filled with hope, courage and the strength of a new life.

On a Sunday morning, I got a cup of coffee and was ready to sit down in front of the television. The phone rang. A friend from my church called me and she told me to turn on the TV, Channel 56. The station was Michigan Public Broadcasting; she said that I would be interesting in hearing about what he was saying. The speaker was Dr. Deepak Chopra, M.D., who studied Eastern medicine. He was explaining how human consciousness leads to total freedom of living the way we wanted to, but also, the higher mind, or higher consciousness of human mind, could create unconditional love. He added, if all humans lived in this kind of consciousness, there would be much more things to offer ourselves and others as well, becoming true spiritual beings. As their consciousness grows, all humans can use their wisdom, (but also, the unlimited potential of human vitality) to make themselves and the world better.

I was astonished. I had the quench for the knowledge and thirsty for why I was planted on the Earth. I readily absorbed what he was saying and the quest for a spiritual journey. It was something new and mysterious. Right away, something pushed me impulsively and my mind was moved by this doctor. Nevertheless, I was remembering what Thomas said about how I'd found the Lutheran church. As soon as the program ended, I had to go to the bookstore and look for his book. Of course, I couldn't speak well so I had a hard time asking for the book by name. I kept looking for the book without anyone's help, and something caught my eye. The book literally jumped into my hands. The title was *One Way Relationship: When You Love Them More Than They Love You.* It was a long title but I grabbed the book immediately. I brought it home and started reading. Page after page, the book was filled with information that related to my past. I had 30 some years of emotional garbage lodged deep in my heart and it begin to stir up. The way the author wrote was easy for me to understand, and the knowledge I received from it was phenomenal. I did not know I had a gift.

I read a total of three hundred pages over eight hours. The author wrote his book in the sense of the Bible because it contained Psalm 23, "The Lord is my shepherd . . ." I finished reading, and also looked up my Bible. After I had been baptized, the pastor of my church gave a Bible to me. I read the Bible and sat for a while. I realized that I had been a victim of my own culture, a cultural barrier which I had suppressed in marriage but also one I had not hadn't crossed for thirty-eight years. I finally found myself weeping hard as I could. Whatever the reason, I wanted to find and free myself. I knew my life had much to offer but how to start was the question. In my life, no human had touched like this book did. I thought Kevin touched me in a way better than my ex-husband did, but he hadn't, after all. I devoted my life honestly and had worked hard but what made me go through such an unspeakable hardship that I had to endure? I only wanted to be a good person, find the perfect love that I deserved, and yet, I never found it.

As I wept for many hours I had a sudden realization. There would be more hardships to come but I would beat them. I decided I needed to spiritually cleanse myself to become a truly whole being and I wanted to become a true spiritual being. I wanted to experience whatever being a true spiritual being meant.

In my life there were many deep roots of past traumas which had to heal. Therefore, in every relationship I had I was looking for perfect intimacy, but I did not know what that was. I tried to care about more people at any cost. The more I cared for those people, they always hurt me. I'd tried to kill myself four times but I couldn't die. My final conclusion was I must heal myself, and in order to heal, I had to start from a baby step. I wanted to love myself and be loved by someone.

I had gotten to the bottom of the problem in me and I wanted to dig deeper. I was whispering to myself, *If there is someone who could touch me the deepest inner being I would be with that person forever, and if, I would find that person, I would live my life faithfully and would have a devoted relationship.* It was self-assuring thought. The night came and I soaked my pillow with tears. That night I prayed, "Please God help me to heal the wounds in my heart. I am too tired of living now. So, please help me, hold me tight in your arms and don't let me fall again. I have sinned, please forgive my sin and forgive those who have hurt me before."

That night, it was the first prayer with tears and the day was June 15, 1996. I had a dream like a nightmare but it was different. It had series of events and each time I woke up I had to write them down and then go back to sleep. I will never forget those dreams for as long as I live.

In the dreams, I was walking up a hill and stood against the wind. The weather was gloomy and the wind was so strong it was lifting up the dirt. On the hill, there was nothing that could stop the wind because there were no trees. As the wind picked up the dirt, it threw it onto my back and I could actually feel the hurt even in dream. I was looking around and I wasn't alone. There were many ordinary people standing on the hill. They were Black, White, Asian; old, young, women, and men. All those people were standing together throwing rocks at four women riding the horses. The four women riding the horses were beating the people with black whips. The women were all dressed old fashioned, like in the movie, "Gone with the Wind." One of the women got down from the horse and sat on a huge rock where the people were standing. I saw her face and she was dark and gloomy. She was a rich woman looking at her clothes but I remember her face vividly. Then the scene had changed. I was ready to leave the hill; a black woman asked me what my name was. I said to her, "My name is Kay." She told me that she would like to plant a tree for me. I thought to myself, Why does she want to plant a tree?

I was finally ready to leave, but something caught my eye. I looked down; there was a modern style building, gray and square like some kind of office building. I was curious and went down the hill. I was sliding, kicking up the dirt, and there were a few bushes and tall wild grass that I could hold on and slide down all the way. When I got down to the building, I saw a window was open, and with my curiosity, I had to peek inside. I saw a man sitting on a chair at the desk and he was facing one the hill. He was wearing a black clerical collar shirt, like a priest. He was between 40-50 years old. On his desk, there was a Japanese apricot tree placed in a glass vase and it had bloomed beautifully. The colors were peach and white with blended pinkish flowers. It was so gorgeous. I attempted to take the vase, but the man at the desk said, "I know what you want, but you cannot have it because it is not your time yet." When I heard this, I felt a chilliness creep over my body. I felt that my body was tense and my throat was dry. He knew exactly why I had come down the hill.

He ordered me to go up the hill. I was discouraged and sort of angry at myself. Nevertheless, I went back up the hill, but everyone was gone. All of sudden, I remembered what the black woman said. She would plant a tree for me and I wanted to find that tree. I was looking around and saw a stump of a tree. The stump was about two foot high and it was growing out of tiny cracks in the asphalt without leaves. Instantly, I knew the tree was mine. Somehow I had peace in my heart that a tree would grow because it had my name on it. I looked toward that tree once more and I finally left the hills.

The weather was bright and I walked a long way. I turned my head; I saw a bus was coming toward me. I stopped the bus and the door was opened. I hopped on the bus. I realized there was no one else on the bus, and yet, the bus was still moving and saw the freeway. The freeway way was curved and it divided. The right curve was sunny and bright, the left curve was gloomy and foggy. The bus took me to the left curve into the fog. The road was a narrow and the bus door was opened. I got off the bus and walked again. The road I took eventually led me into a tunnel, and as I walked in, I could not see much. It was pitch dark but straight, far ahead, there was a dingy strip of light I could see. In my thoughts, I just needed follow that light. I walked a little way into the tunnel and I saw a big hole. The hole was about the size of a human body; length, width depth of a casket. As I passed a few feet more, I noticed there was a kind of blanket over the hole, and by the side of the blanket, there was a T-shirt folded in a triangle. I could not see clearly what it was at first. Then, when I looked again, the T-shirt had an eagle printed on it and the colors were blue, red, and white. I did see what it was and I was satisfied. I was moving forward. As I was walking away, I didn't think much about anything. I just wanted to get out of that place. I kept on walking for a minute or two.

Suddenly, I had a hunch that someone or something was following me. I looked back. I could see a human-like form, but it was not human. In my knowledge, the thing we could see in the horror movie. It had a square face and its body was covered with blood. It was a skinny, dirty, naked body; it had only the bone but no meat. I noticed the form was following me as fast as it could. I was scared and I started to run but how far was it to that strip of light? I had no idea. I had two choices: either I kept running toward the light or go straight up. There was no time for me to even think so I decided to go up. I was scared of dying in the tunnel. I stopped running and touched the rough tunnel walls. It was dark, but I was determined to climb up. There was not much support on my feet because the tunnel was manmade but I found that it was rough. I knew I could hold the rough areas of the wall and something was sticking out for me to put up the one foot. I kept climbing and soon there would be something, and my foot never slid on the walls. I was almost reaching the ceiling and I saw very little light from the ceiling of the tunnel. I thought it was light but it wasn't as I got closer to the top. The top of the ceiling had four layers of windows which were not made of glass. They were wood, like an old farmhouse in the back of the house for safe place to hide and I had to open one layer after another. As each layer had opened, more light came into the tunnel.

I opened the fourth layer and I saw the sunlight, the blue sky and many more surprises waiting for me. There was a man standing nearby and he reached for my hand vigorously. He pulled my whole body from hanging on the wall. He was a handsome white man wearing an orange colored robe. He never spoke. There was white woman with short brunette hair appearing from somewhere and she told us to follow her. The man was behind me and the woman was in front of me. They were protecting me for some reason, I thought. She guided us into the white building. The man had gone but in the building there was another woman was waiting for us. The brunette haired woman was talking with another woman. She was wearing a white dress which looked like a Korean folk dress. She looked so gorgeous. She was unusually calm and from her smile I knew I could trust her.

She asked me to follow her again. As I followed her, I was counting how many doors I had been passing and she stopped at the fourth door. I entered into the room and looked around. All four walls were white brick, and it looked like the home in which I grew up in Korea, but one part of the wall was cut out in a diamond shape

205

which also had four lines. I was curious about where I was and I looked around through the hole. I was shocked because the thing I saw in the tunnel was in the building. I was terrified again and lay down on the cement floor, trying not to breathe. The floor was smooth. I knew I had touched this kind of floor before. Nevertheless, my attention was focused on the wall from the other side. The lady brought me into the room was outside and she spoke to the thing. "She isn't here, you come with me." She had spoken softly, gently and politely. The woman diverted the thing's attention from me. She was skillful and had great patience.

A few minutes passed, and I was still lying on the floor. My body was getting chilled and I noticed I was wearing a dress like the woman, a white Korean folk dress. The lady came into the room and said, "Kay, get up. He is gone." She touched my left thigh. I was crouched on the floor like a duck and it hurt. I slowly changed body position and managed to look at the details of her figure. She was beautiful like a lilly, the flower I love so much, and her charm could lead me to somewhere beautiful. She had small figure like me, and dark hair.

As she touched my thigh, I woke up with a scream. "Oh my God, there is an angel!"

Nineteen

As I woke up I touched my thigh. I knew someone or something had touched the lower part of my left thigh. It was like when my mom touched me on my right lower arm. I was astonished by what I experienced through the dream. What a magnificent dream I had had but it was different than any other. I got up and looked at the clock. It was 8:00 a.m. and I had to get ready to work. As I pushed open the glass door of my apartment, I felt somehow different than usual. In my mind I had a random guess that something was very wrong. I felt extremely awkward. I sensed that I could fly because my body had no weight and there was lightness on my shoulders. The sky was unbelievably clearer than any of the day I had seen before. I felt that something had stopped, like the world wasn't turning anymore. I was so happy. A few days went by and I was anxious to tell someone but how? I was an inexperienced person in human life, especially like an angel. I was nervous and my body could not rest at night. If I told people they might think I was crazy and I did not like to hear the word "crazy."

I called my therapist. She asked me to come to see her. I talked her about what happened in my dream. She said to just accept it because in the world there is more than just us. I did not understand what she was saying. She did not help me, so why I did come to see her? I knew I wasn't crazy. I had to prove it to myself. I had constant thoughts about the dream.

Finally, I decided talk to someone who was religious all her life. She was Catholic and she worked with youth in the church. I believed that she would tell me something that was mysterious, and she was an open-minded person, I thought. I told her about my dream and how I had physically changed internally, the way I felt, and so on.

She couldn't tell me much but she thought that my burden had been lifted by God. Her answer was broad. It wasn't the answer I was looking for and it made me feel stupid so I kept my mouth shut. Sometimes I had a personality like a child and when I wasn't satisfied with what I wanted to hear I usually got bored very easily. I needed a better explanation and I had to be sure about who God was.

In the end of June, 1996 one of my clients who worked in the Catholic Church and her friend were leaving the United States to go to Korea to pick up a child for adoption. My guess was that it was some kind of international program about adopting children from Korea; but I would not know because I didn't speak well enough to understand all of it. The couple who would be bringing the child to the United States asked me if I had any family members or friends who lived in Korea. I told them I had a friend but I did not have my family and even if I did I did not know where my sisters were. Diane and Thomas asked me to give them my friend's phone number. They didn't mind delivering letters or pictures for me and when they got to Korea, they would call my friend. I hadn't thought about Mrs. Park and her daughter, Won Ae. I hadn't thought about Won Ae for awhile because of the divorce and my life was a total mess. After the divorce, when I chose life instead of death, I cut off all letters and suddenly I missed her. I wanted to let her know that I was alright. Besides, I hadn't thought about any of my sisters for years since my mother passed away. I gave my letter, phone number, and pictures of what I looked like.

Within a week, I had a phone call from Won Ae. I was surprised and tears rolled down my face. I was relieved. Won Ae told me that all four of them met, Won Ae's husband and the couple I knew. Won Ae told me she would be seeing me because she would be attending a wedding ceremony in New York State. She would like to meet me before the wedding and would stop in Michigan before going to New York. Surprisingly, there was another phenomenon: my sister was looking for me in Korea at the same time. My sister came to see Won Ae and asked where I was and she would be bringing my sister's letter and asked me what I wanted from Korea. I told her I wanted to have a Korean folk dress. It was the only thing I had an attachment to and my sister would send it to Won Ae. It was another miracle from God and I did not know what to make of all this craziness in my life.

I was up and down like a child just learning to walk one step toward his or her parents, and yet, at the same time I had unstoppable tears that I couldn't control. All the years of suppressed, hardened emotions were melting like winter snow. The last time I saw her was Mom's funeral in 1982. It was her choice not to see me because she was embarrassed about what I did for living. It wasn't my choice the way I had lived. At the funeral I was hurt again because my own flesh and blood didn't want to accept me as a human.

My sister called me where I worked. The lady who answered the phone asked my sister how she knew me and my sister told that I was her friend instead her sister. My sister was 3,000 miles away and through the phone line we were connected again. It was an unbelievably odd event. We were on opposite ends of the earth from each other but we were together at the same time. I had goose bumps all over. Won Ae explained to my sister because I couldn't speak Korean at all any more. Won Ae spoke English. It took me nine years to forget my own language but I did understand their conversation. We were on the phone for about an hour but the only words I spoke were "Oh, oh . . ." and how awesome God was. My heart was pounding. I could hear my own heartbeat. My blood was pumping faster than a racecar engine. Tears were rolling down my face like a dam that had burst.

Somehow we said goodbye to each other, and soon, Won Ae would be seeing me. In the meantime, I had to find someone who could drive me to the airport. Since I came to the United States in 1987 I had never been to the airport, besides, I was still scared of driving on the freeway and most areas were still new to me. I contacted Thomas and explained to him what had been happening and I needed his help. Thomas agreed to take me to the airport and bring Won Ae and he would take her back to the airport. Thomas never saw Won Ae but she saw him in the photograph from our wedding in 1987. It was very nice of him even after our divorce.

Won Ae finally arrived at night. At first, I couldn't remember her face. She was older and her dark skin got darker than when she was her 20's. I realized that everyone had been changing but I didn't think I had been changing much at all. Matter of fact, I just got younger and I was full of hope and strength. I did not know where my strength was coming from, for surely I had lived another thousand years. Won Ae recognized me right away even though she hadn't seen me in nine long years. Thomas introduced himself to her and she thanked him for picking her up.

Won Ae asked me in Korean, "Hey, Kyong Mi, how could both of you still be a friend even after divorce?" I mumbled. I'd loved to explain to her why, but I could not. I'd completely lost my own language, and I struggled with expressing my thoughts in English. She broke the silence. She told me I was the same as when I left Korea in 1987, and thanked Thomas for being so kind- hearted to me even after the divorce. On the way to my apartment, we stopped at the restaurant and had an early breakfast together.

Thomas dropped us off at 2:00 a.m. Won Ae did not have energy to talk to me because she had to leave the same afternoon for the next day wedding in New York. She told me that she could not erase thinking about me since the visitation from that American couple in the hotel lobby in Seoul. Her foremost concern was that I had attempted numerous suicides while I was young, but when she saw my apartment, she did not worry about me anymore. She opened her luggage and gave me the Korean folk dress from my sister, a few letters, pictures. There were pictures of my grandmother, aunt and her kids who had been married and her grandson and daughter. My sister got married and had a son also. My two other sisters also had a few kids.

What an eccentric and mysterious life story I saw through those pictures. I was looking through these pictures and viewing my past; we hadn't been together for over thirty years. My other two sisters looked different, even though they're twins. According to my sister's letter, the twins got married to good men and their families were good to the twin sisters. The twins never went to school and they didn't know how to read or write. After my father passed away, we didn't have the money to go to school, except I was the fortunate one because at least I knew how to write or read. At least, I went to 3rd grade and had to stop.

We wanted to talk more but she had to catch up on a few hours of sleep. We were quickly wrapping up with stories that my sister remembered the most and how my mom hit me all the time. I was a good sister but she remembered me as being very stubborn. Won Ae went to bed. I was crying silently. I was looking for my baby sister's pictures but I was disappointed. My darling sister, the only time I held her was at my father's funeral. My sister's letter said that she tried finding me but she gave up. It was painful to look at those pictures. I was thinking, *What would it be like when I was ready to go to searching for my siblings in Korea?* I had to put all pictures and letters away. I thought I was happy to see my sisters but it made me shed more tears than I had ever experienced in my life. I was overwhelmed by all the things that happened since I was baptized. I realized that too many sad memories were stored in the back of my mind. It was a matter of time before I exploded.

Won Ae woke up. She knew I hadn't slept all night. It was a

lot to swallow at once. That afternoon, Thomas came to pick her up and took her to the airport. I said goodbye to her and that was the last time I spoke with her. I sent her a thank you note, but I never received anything back from her. I felt that it was the first miracle God performed and I felt that I was never going to see Won Ae again because it was her purpose and her work was done for me.

After Won Ae left, Thomas' family visited me for his birthday. I invited them with Thomas' girlfriend. She was a nice person. We could easily share our conversation at the dinner table. Her birthday was a few days before mine and I thought that he had learned something from her too. In my heart, he would be happy with her and hoping that would share happiness with her. I knew if I had grown up in a different environment, had an education and different life experience I could had been living with Thomas rest of my life. It was the first time I was truly thankful with my life and especially to Thomas for bringing me to the United States. We had a great time being together, and before they left, Thomas asked me if I wanted to go with them to see a play at the Masonic Temple. I had never been to a play before and I wanted to go with them.

The play was "Miss Saigon" so we set up for our schedule to meet again. The day came to go to The Masonic Temple and I was wearing a Korean folk dress which my sister got for me. The color was lavender and it had embroidered patterns of daisies and butterflies; the material was a mixture of silk and nylon. I certainly did not feel uncomfortable, and in fact, I felt that for the first time in my life I saw myself in truth. I realized it was true that I had hated myself so much. I could no longer deny it anymore. On the street, in front of the theater, people were looking at me like they had never seen any Korean before. For the first time there was no shame in being Korean. The three of us went into the theater, and Thomas was sitting in the middle of us. I remembered the past with Kevin but I immobilized that thought instantly. The play would be starting

212

in 15 minutes and I did not want to spoil a good time with the man I once had in my life. Thomas was a good host, and his girlfriend was, too. The first part of the play, I was looking at myself. It was a familiar story in which the main character met her husband and how her life had changed; then in the end, she actually died. I had tears and I could not stop crying even though his girlfriend was next to him. I felt that someone had stabbed the knife into my chest and scooped out all of my guts. I questioned myself, "Why?" I know I disturbed the people around me but seeing the character as myself, I had different view of life. I remembered that Kevin had asked me "Why?" I now know why he asked me that.

The play had conveyed to me more a sense of who I was and I declared again, "I will never, ever try to kill myself again." Thomas watched me, and he rubbed my back. It was his expression for he was still cared about me but I did not have love for him. Thomas and I had a different kind of love. I was still searching for a love that could fulfill me to the end of my life. I wanted an absolutely perfect, unconditional love that was so true. I did want to find it.

Thomas and his girlfriend dropped me off at my apartment and he told me if I needed to talk I could call him. I know he was sorry for me but it was alright because actually our friendship got better than before. Each day, I was getting happier and I had forgiven Kevin and the letters I had been sent also stopped. I was getting my act together and continued to learn what I had to learn; whether it was from books, movies, or music. I was encountering all sorts of people and maybe I talked to them about my dreams.

Everyday, in each house I went to work in, there was something happening. I could not explain what was happening. For example, I saw my client in my dream and she had a fire. My schedule for cleaning her house was a week away, but I went out of my way to stop at her house, and warn her about the fire I saw in my dream. My client said that I was crazy and it was just a dream. She had been ignoring me many times, but that morning, she found her iron was plugged in an electrical outlet, and it was turned on. She said that no one had been using her iron but the iron was burning hot. The gas stove was on with a pot without water in it. She was a client but I did not like her because she did not trust me. She thought it was strange and yet, she doubted about my dream. I was frustrated with my dreams and I could not get enough rest at night, but I was able to get up and function everyday smoothly. I felt that someone or something inside me all the time and did all the work for me. I did not get angry whatever people said or did. I was just a happy baby.

It had been a hectic month of July. I had no memory of how July went by and before the month's end I decided to go on a camping trip in Grayling alone. I had never done this before but I thought I had courage. In my wildest thought, I worried that if I got lost somewhere in the woods, someone would find me. I had determination. I had camping equipment from Thomas when I got divorced and it had been sitting around in the storage room for some time. I told my friend where I was going and her concern was if I was going to be okay. I told her I just needed to rest and it would be a good adventure without a man. I packed up my canvas, paint and brush, and also I should not forget my fishing poles, wader, boots, and all camping equipment. I had to buy a new tent. I was all set to leave my apartment on July 21st after work. My cat Willy had enough food and water but just in case, I told my friend to stop by my home awhile I was away.

On Friday afternoon, I was on the freeway for the first time. It was a long trip alone but I felt that someone was with me all the way. I had confidence and I did not think about anything anymore except, every once in awhile, I had reflection of what it was like before while I was married. The most recent memory I had was that last camping trip with the three of us, Kevin, Thomas and me. I drove three and half hours alone without stopping anywhere. I came to downtown Grayling and I had to stop at the gas station. I filled up the gas tank and I asked the clerk how I could find the Manistee campgrounds.

Politely, he explained every detail about how to get there. I knew there was something in me guiding me this far. I arrived at the sunset and before get dark, I set the tent up first. I figured that as long as the stakes were in the ground I was safe, and next, I walked over to the river bank where Kevin took the picture of me. Along the river, everything was still standing motionlessly, the fence, the pine trees and Kevin's smile. The only thing changed was I was alone.

I missed Kevin, but at this moment, I was with him in this place with his spirit. I did not know it was me or someone acting like me. I was simply reflecting the time I had left and the moment I shared with him endlessly. I had tears. Kevin was still lingering everywhere but I did not know how shake him off. Every breath I took, he was in and out with me. I leaned on the pine tree and I saw Kevin right next to me, holding my hand. He held my shoulders gently and pulled me into his chest. He was my man. He was some kind of hero still living with me and he did not know when he would be leaving me. I hugged the pine tree and said told that Kevin to be with me someday. I came to my tent and cooked for my dinner. I did not need a lot. I made a few cups of coffee and maybe a can of soup. Next to me, I had company which I had not seen when I first arrived. These people walked over to me and introduced themselves and told me that if I needed something to come see them. They were elderly people but seemed to me super nice. They said that their son and daughter would visit in the morning and we planned on having breakfast together. I told them that it was nice of them and I was planning on seeing them in the morning. I was grateful because I met someone out of nowhere. I thought, at least, I had someone to talk to while I was in this quiet place.

It was getting really late but I could not close my eyes. All night long, I was having dreams that meaningful and spiritual aspect but I had no idea what I could make up of. Finally, the morning had arrived. I decided to walk. I wanted to enjoy every moment while there was an opportunity. I was in the moment of pleasure of breathing the fresh air, and the trails that led me to plenty of pine trees in the deep forest. In the forest, each tree gave me fresh oxygen and it cleaned my throat and my entire body. In this place not only did I find some joy in my life but also, I found amusement for my eyes. In this place, I saw nature's morning activities. Those activities were full of caring and innocent pure acts. In that quiet morning, just about sunrise, a herd of deer were running through the woods and others were standing by the creek sipping the fresh water. Then the noisy birds were loudly chirping away welcoming the beautiful morning. I was wondering what else was living in the woods, and would these creatures remember me like I remembered them? I felt that those creatures were talking to me like my best friend and said that "Come on Kay, we will guide you to a place where you will be happy always." I was seeing the nature in the most precious moments of my free time and the most amazing place. I walked around all the way up the stream and down stream and it was about a mile and a half.

I returned to my tent and my neighbor was waiting for me to have breakfast. I introduced myself to the elderly couple's son and daughter-in-law. We shared the breakfast and they told me that we would share the evening when I returned from fishing. I traveled the upper Manistee River along the bank and when I found shallow water, I walked the river. I was catching a few native brown trout and brook trout but most of them were small. I spent the entire morning to catch one fish which big enough to cook. I didn't have much in the cooler because I figured that if I caught enough fish, I did not have to buy a lot of food but I wanted to go to the store and I needed to pick up a few things. Also, I wanted to get something for my neighbor because they had been feeding me two meals and at least, I show them my gratitude.

I went to the store in downtown Grayling. I passed the lake. It was a very familiar place; white sand, pine trees, the church and the hotel. I did not remember clearly. I felt that everything I had experienced in this place so long ago was like a dream and it was a story that I had lived. I realized I had been changed, but not the place. The place welcomed me but I did not feel I wanted to be there. I realized that it was the last time I would ever be in this town, and I glanced at it one last time.

I picked up a few things; milk, orange juice and bread. Suddenly, I was hungry for a peanut butter and jelly sandwich. I got into the campground but I did not see where I was going and got stuck in the sand bar. I panicked. I did not know how to operate a brand new Jeep. It was about 3 o'clock and I had to find someone to get my Jeep out of from the sand bar. I saw a woman driving in my direction and stopped her. I explained to her what my situation was and I needed someone to help me. The woman told me she would send someone and wait in the car. My helpers arrived. There were four men and all of them were friends enjoying a weekend camping trip. They thought it was different because I was a foreigner who did not speak well but brave enough to travel alone. One of them pulled my vehicle out of the sand bar and showed me an instruction page on what to do if the situation happened again. I thanked them and I planned on visiting them by evening. My car was free and I went back to the store again. I bought a few cases of six packs and came back to my place. I freshened up and visited them before it got dark.

When I got there, there were more than four guys. They had their girlfriends and were having a good time. They were talking about how my car was in the sand bar. It was too dark to take their pictures so I asked them I could take pictures of them next morning. I used to be afraid of a lot of men but I did not scare anymore, at least with these guys. I left them with six packs. On the way to my place, I thought, I would paint tomorrow by the river. I thought about how I came to the United States. I did not remember what July 21st was and without remembering I was living day by day. The pain was still lingering in the back of my head without healing the wounds in my heart.

It was around August 1996 and there was a dream about Thomas and my baby sister. *I was wearing white clothes and carrying my baby sister on my back. I was standing in an alley behind the house. The house was built with white brick and on the wall there was only one window, and a few feet away there was a streetlight. The color of the atmosphere was dark grayish blue, and I leaned on the street light pole. There a man came to me. He wanted to see me inside a home. I let my sister on my bed. This man held me to have sex with me but I did not like the man. I was struggling to get away from him but I could not. My sister was crying and I had to get to her but I did not know how. He held my right wrists so tight and I felt the pain. I finally pushed him and got off the bed.*

When I awoke from the dream I had a hurting sensation on my wrist. I gazed at my wrist first, and sure enough my wrist had red marks of a man's hand and I knew right away that the hand was Thomas'. I wanted to have an answer for why I had married. I wasn't sure what love was but my marriage went on for 10 years. I felt that was the right answer that I was looking for and finally I could rest that part. I had conviction. My conclusion of that marriage was simple. Thomas was lonely while he was in Korea and he was 21 years old. He needed a woman to walk with him in his maturity. Whether he had enough sex with me or not, it was the most important part of his life he had to release but he could not. The time we were in Korea, he took all my frustrations without any complaint. The only reason I came with him here was because there were many more things that I had to do.

In the United States, both of us went through our battles but he could not hold me anymore. The only way he could get out of our marriage was to shut down emotions and live the best way we could in order to have his freedom. I remembered that he waited for me to get American citizenship. By the time I had surgery, Kevin came into our marriage. It was a perfect solution for Thomas because my attention was with Kevin and it made him feel that the burden was lifted.

I was analyzing professionally without any degree in detective work. I was satisfied. All puzzles had been put together and I completed the work. I would be able to free myself from the awful experience with Thomas. It wasn't his fault or my fault. We had battled and we both lost. In a moment of silence, I prayed for Thomas. Whatever the reason, I was in this country and I would work much harder and I would make it to the top. I promised that I would always remember what I had experienced with Thomas and Kevin and I would never make the same mistakes ever again if I had another marriage. My dream had been like I was watching a mysterious movie every night. It was a strange dream, but I was living in it.

I received two letters from Kevin. One was on September 6, 1996 and November 2nd of the same year. His first letter indicated that he had a girlfriend and he was plan on leaving Michigan. My guess was that he was scared of me. I realized from his letter he was just a baby and he needed to grow up. I sent him a letter stating that whatever he thought of me, I was simply a good friend and would remain a good friend. I wished him his happiness and God's blessing. I did not trust him. He was a liar because he wanted to get rid of me like Thomas. I had hope. I prayed. I knew I would be happy with a person somewhat like both Thomas and Kevin. All my life, I searched for one thing – love. This love would be so special that it would never fade away from my heart. This love would be so strong that it would not hide in my heart unnoticed. This love would hold me for rest of my life. I'd created a bond between Kevin and me, but it was my time to let him go.

In late fall, I received a second letter from Kevin. His letter said that he was in California and he had fallen in love with a woman and he was very happy. He also said that I found my strength from the Lord and he didn't think I needed him any more. I waited Kevin for over two years. I'd hoped that he would return. I waited for him without knowing what faith was because that was what he taught me. The last letter I received was in November; it actually tore my heart apart but I did not cry. It was just a little tear and I spent most of the day in Oxford Michigan on the lake and I returned to my apartment late in the afternoon.

On my way home, I thought that in this world there was no such special love. I tasted the bitterness in my mouth but it wasn't bad. I thought how twisted friendship was. I always wanted to have a man as a good friend and I thought that I had found it. One friendship was so strong I mixed my feelings, sex and guilt into one and I gave my life for it; but finally realized that I was worth more than Kevin. I did not betray or ruin his friendship but he did it to himself. We all had to take our responsibility but he did not. I was a good woman and I always would be. I actually reflect upon what was right and wrong.

I kept the good part of the wonderful friendship I shared with Kevin, and if there was another chance we'd meet again, I would ask him that what kind of lessons he had learned from me. I would not forget the good memories because he was the first person who taught me what love could be. For me, if I ever see him again, I will thank him for teaching me what love was and for being there when I fell. I had received unconditional moral support from him in the beginning. If I had concealed the truth about us to Thomas, I would not have the kind of freedom I imagined. Therefore, I closed the chapter on Kevin, and hoped that time would heal the wounds and set him free from my heart forever.

Twenty

I felt that someone had been with me for some reason without physical contact. There was something inside me directing my daily life. I did not have to think about anything in life but only the three things: work, painting and meditation. I knew if I wanted to survive I must work harder than before, and painting was my only hobby. Every morning and evening I had been devoted with daily meditations and prayers for my inner growth. My dreams continued and I had not known all the meanings of them but I just knew someday I'd figure it out. I knew there was my purpose. My experience was truly unreal, but how I was going to use it was my choice.

I made the decision for using my gift. I knew I was a different person and I did not like what I was doing for a living. There should be more to life than what I saw through my eyes. There was a bigger and better thing for me to do in this world before I left the Earth. If my dreams appeared in daily life, I had to know why. I talked to my dear friend from church about how I felt, how light I was feeling and seeing things in the air without a microscope. She did not give me a whole lot of answers but she mentioned "Footprints." She told me that God had been carrying me in trust. It was the story of God making each of our journeys a little easier. I understood that whatever happened, I had to trust and faithfully walk at my own pace. There was a lot to learn but I would not rush into it, but walk slowly and faithfully so that I would never miss anything that life could offer. I had already missed too many good things.

I realized that I have a soul and live my life as my soul's purpose. I had experienced all the bad or evil people for my whole life, and I wanted to change with God. I wanted to have a true God experience. It meant that I was not changing physically but shifting my thoughts and my actions toward people and myself as my God-given soul's purpose.

The days went gone by with seemingly impossible tasks but I was completing them without complaint. At the same time I was good to myself because I deserved it. Maybe it was my time to know how to treat myself with respect and love. If there was the day I wanted to do nothing, I was hanging around at home reading a book or listening to music or going fishing. I was totally alone but it was fine. It had been about five months since I had a spiritual experience. Seemingly, I was moving fast everyday like everybody else, but I felt that I was moving five years ahead of everybody else. My body was the same but my mind had been expressing the great details of the inner world through dreams. My inner world shifted in high gear and I had been keeping up with it as fast as I could.

Then something happened. I was driving down a country road and I felt that there was something in my eyes. It was not a thing that I could hold but something that I had never experienced before and it made me uncomfortable. It looked like a diamond shape and very clear. It looked like crystal and had many colors. I felt that my eyes were so heavy and I could not see straight or I could not focus my eyes on the road. I kept rubbing my eyes but it wouldn't go away. Then, I started seeing in double and triple vision. Sometimes, I had to stop because my eyes became blurred and I could not see the traffic light clearly. I returned home right away because I didn't think I should be on the road in that condition. When I returned home, I closed my eyes. I thought that I was tired. When I closed my eyes it went away, and when I opened my eyes it came back. The next morning same thing happened again but I had to go to work. I was driving everywhere in this condition for a few days. It was like broken glass in my eyes transferring the colors from the sun.

On Sunday morning I had to attend Sunday service but during the pastor's sermon, I could not see his face or the congregation. When I was got out of church, I had to walk very slowly because I could not clearly see at all. When I got back from church service, I was watching TV, and suddenly I could not see the words and the entire house—goods in my apartment seemed to be falling into my eyes. I was really scared, and called my friend to drive me to the hospital emergency. In the emergency room many hours later, the doctor could not find anything wrong with me. My eyes were normal but my blood pressure was high. The doctor said that high blood pressure could cause the eyes to act up and he said to take it easy. I did not believe what the doctor said, and on Monday I called my doctor. He also couldn't find anything wrong with me. I knew that I was a healthy person. I wasn't blind but I lived like blind woman for three days and three nights. On the fourth day, my vision returned to normal and I could see clearer than usual. I felt that I had a brand new and fresh feeling in my eyes.

Since I missed a few days of work, my clients' houses were messy again because most of their children were messy. I loved these children but they were messy. These children were between eight and twelve years old, and most of the clients were really appreciating my hard work and I began to accept their appreciation. I was thanking them for their kindness and they kept me as part of their families. Anything I wanted to eat or drink while I was working was alright. I had freedom and I was growing like a little kid. I was re-entering my youth in a different way but I did not know how to behave. I was a simple, ignorant and uneducated foreigner.

It was late September, and something really happened that almost killed me in the basement of a client's home. In this home, I had to work eight hours a day once a week. It was about lunch time and I hadn't eaten. I passed the laundry room and opened up the refrigerator door. I could not find anything for me to eat. In a glass fruit bowl, I saw a delicious red apple. It looked tempting so I grabbed it and had one bite. All of a sudden, I had a stomach ache and I could not even move. I lay down for a while but the pain in my stomach wouldn't go away. I almost called emergency but the pain suddenly disappeared.

The same afternoon, I was down in the basement. I had just passed a counter where the bar was and I lowered my back behind the counter. In short, all the liquor on display on the glass shelves fell down disastrously and ruined about 20 bottles of drinks. Again, I was scared and I did not really understand. I was worrying about if I had to pay—I did not have money. They had expensive things but probably a lot of money. When the homeowner returned from work, I explained it to her. She said that it was just drink and told me not to worry about it. I was thinking, *If this would have happened in Korea I could had been beaten.*

This country was different from Korea. I was beginning to like people and gained their trust but I had a hard time trusting these people, especially women. The reason I did not trust woman because I thought about my mother so often. I felt that my mother had been following me everywhere I went. Whenever I remembered my mother, I went outside and sat on the bench and looked at the trees and at the river behind the house. It was a peaceful, serene view. I could hear the sound of falling leaves and as it fell, blowing wind made the leaves rubbing together. Maybe they liked to race each other saying, "I want to get down there first." I knew all things had their own purpose and I would find mine from talking to nature. Connecting with nature was my gift, and I was fascinated by its wonders.

My client who was an interior designer introduced me to another client in Rochester. I decided to work in her home once a week. It was September 21, 1996. The owner had a huge home but only two people living in it and a cat. I thought, *How nice!* This home reminded me of Mrs. Park. The floor was marble and wood, and the decorations reminded me of ancient Rome or Greece. I was working about two or three weeks, and beginning to get comfortable with this new client. The new client liked the way I worked and I trusted her like Mrs. Park. I hardly ever saw her husband. I knew her husband owned the company in Rochester and he traveled a lot, and in fact, she was going out of town when I got there on the 21st. She was different. She never spoke loud, never complained about how I worked. I was always on time and never missed work. Seemed to me all my clients were happy people and I was heading somewhere with these clients on a spiritual journey yet to be appear.

I stopped painting and I decided to go back to school. I took a class about teaching how to manage money. I was making enough money but it seemed to me I did not know how important money was and I did not know how to save. The teacher explained about credit card debt and how it was catching up with my life. It made me to think how important it was for me to start saving money. It was an important thing for me to remember, and I opened my savings account. I took another class and this time I met a teacher who I had previously at the Adult Ed in Livonia, Michigan in 1991. I felt that something really strange was at work because things were happening again and again. I was meeting the same people again and having identical experiences. My new teacher was fascinated by my story. He said that what I had experienced was awesome. The depth of my soul was opened; the subconscious of my inner being was being answered.

The time had been passed quickly and it was end of September, 1996. I had been receiving annoyance calls from someone. It was the man who had helped me while I was in the process of divorcing, the man who brought my sewing machine to the motel. I was thankful when he helped me so I took him to dinner once, and I met him a few times. I did not like him, though. After I had my spiritual experience, he called me and wanted to see me many times. I didn't want to. Each time he called me I hung up as nicely as I could be but he'd kept calling. This made me uncomfortable so I reported it to the police. The policeman gave me a case number and the Ameritech annoyance bureau would trace all the calls coming into my apartment. It had been a month and I hadn't been received any more annoyance calls. At the end of October, there was a call from the detective bureau. His name was Peter, and he was a detective at the Southfield Police Station. He looked through my file and the case had been opened. He wanted to know I was planned on prosecuting "X'. I told him that I hadn't planned on prosecuting him. He told me that if I was still receiving the annoyance calls to let him know because he was assigned to my case. I told the detective that I knew who the man was. Surprisingly, the detective offered to call the man and tell him not to harass me anymore. I thanked him for his generous offer, but it wouldn't be necessary.

The detective and I were on the phone for awhile even after matter was over. Peter started talking to me about his past in Korea before he got married. He was a Marine who was stationed in Pu San, Korea. That place had plenty of action every day. I thought, *He spent his youth in a great place.* He explained further that he had a Korean girlfriend while stationed in Pu San, but he did not bring her here. I thought, *He may have regret now because talking to me brought him the memory of his ex-girlfriend.* The first day we were on the phone, we shared honestly about what kind of trouble we'd had in our lives. It was another coincidence that both of us shared what our beliefs were. Both of us thought there were many reasons for us to meet someday. Peter and I were then on the phone often. We planned on seeing each other.

It was the second celebration of my birthday after my divorce. I invited a few clients who were becoming my friends. There were about ten people in my small apartment. They wished me a good life with everlasting love from God, and I was speedily recovering from all my painful experiences. I received flowers, books and more as birthday gifts. Then, the policeman called me. I was surprised. I never even dreamed about I would be going out with someone like him. We planned on meeting. He would come to my apartment and pick me up and take me to a Korean restaurant in Southfield. I was excited to see him again. I did not sleep well that night.

Finally, a dream visited me. The dream was vivid, colorful. In the dream, *there were three people in a boat, two women and a man. The man was rowing the boat and the boat was traveling upstream. The older woman was like the mother and a couple was like her son and her daughter- in- law. The man let go of the rowing the boat and came closer to the woman. In the boat, the couple was making love and the mother was watching over them like a guardian. It was a night sky and the full moon was guiding the boat where it was heading. The sky's color was royal blue and golden moonlight was shining on the river. Along the river, the tree branches were hanging like a creepy movie in the broken arms of numerous dead bodies. I was scared. I could see something in the sky but also the old woman saw something in the sky. The elderly woman was talking to a cloud, saying, "Go away." As soon she said that, the man lifted something from his head. I noticed that both of them were wearing some kind of hat, like native Indians wore with and braided hair with ribbons. The man had salt and pepper colored hair and on the end of the braids, there were a set of red ribbons on them. The woman had exactly the same as the man but with blue ribbons. I knew the woman was myself, the man was my future and the old woman was his mother or someone from our past who had been guiding us to the place where they might be.*

I had a clear thought. I woke up to write it down and thought about Peter. Peter was a quiet and compassionate man when we talked over dinner. He talked me about his wife and kids. I realized from our conversation that his marriage was on the rocks and he was looking for a place to let go, even if it was for one night. At the dinner table, he told me that I was different, that I sounded like an uplifting personality and very happy person while we were on the phone. He hadn't seen anyone like me. I had no idea why I was happy, and why he wanted to see me and have dinner.

It was after 10:00 p.m. and beginning to snow. I invited him into my apartment. I hadn't seen a man since Kevin, and I missed a man. It was the only opportunity and I did not want to miss out. David told me that he was in the process of divorce. It was alright for me. I did not plan on doing anything and I was not interested in any deeper relationship. We enjoyed each other and he left me early in the morning. After he left, the same day, I sensed that something had been changed in me. The feeling of fullness since after my baptismal had disappeared. I was devastated. I felt that I lost something valuable in me, and there was a hole in my heart but it wasn't sadness. It was a different feeling than before I became a Christian.

I continued contact with him through letters and cards and about a year and a half later, he came to see me. He told me that he decided to quit his job as policeman. I did not ask why he was quitting his job. I figured out that there was something that he could not discuss. I knew what the reason was. While he was away, I received my vision about him. As a policeman, he wasn't doing well in my vision. In my vision, his police car was splashing through the mud and he was stepping on the brakes as fast as he could. The squad police car was up and down the hills in the mud, but I had not seen his face whole time.

I met Peter twice in 1999 and he told me that he changed jobs and was driving a UPS truck. I realized this man also had something in common with Kevin. Peter had some traits of Kevin, like that unchangeable personality that he had to have his way. He had set on his mind on a certain way. His stubbornness would break my heart if I was plan on staying with him. I could not stay anywhere near a man like that ever again, and it was the one last time we had dinner together. After dinner, he showed me his children's pictures.

His children were riding in the mud racing motorcycles. At least, I was not mean a person and accepted him as who he was. I had no regret and I hope he has learned something from me.

The days were rather passing quickly because many of clients were having Christmas parties and I received an invitation. I wanted to buy a nice dress. In a store in Birmingham I bought a long black velvet dress. It was sleeveless and in the back, there was a ribbon. I tried it on and I looked like a rich woman. I paid $500 for it. At the party, I wore the dress and came down from the upstairs. Friends saw me and said, "Look at you." My client had not seen me like that before. I had never seen a Christmas party like this. All of my clients guests were rich and I was not fit for that crowd but what did I know about social life? It was the introduction to what it could be when I became something more than what I was.

I was busy working during Christmas because everyone wanted to extra cleaning for their homes. I was getting plenty of bonuses from all my clients but it was getting hard on my body. I was the only person but I had a workload of 10 people which was not something very many people could do. I was glad that I was Korean and I had a great work ethic. I was strong but also I had the will to do whatever I had to do, and in addition, I was back in school for getting that GED. I had the load of homework, paying the bills, and took care of house chores. On and off I was mediating because I realized it helped me to function better in my daily life. Through daily meditation, I was getting enough feedback, physically, mentally, and emotionally. All the work I had to do each day, I had to accomplish by myself. Sometimes, frustration had built up inside of me, but I managed nicely through daily meditation. I realized that it gave me comfort and I worried less and less.

I did not know how to meditate because I did not have any training but I had an idea that I must think something was really good to me and it was God. Every night, before I went to bed, I was talking to God to help me get through every day and walk with me the rest of my life. The days were passing smoothly and the New Year had begun. In the middle of January, I went to a holistic doctor in Canton, Michigan. The doctor told me that I had to work less because I was dealing with an overwhelming workload and it might cause problems in my bones. I needed to take better care of myself because my body was a vessel which carries my soul. I had some kind of idea but I wasn't sure what the doctor was talking about. I knew I would be alright because I had my God.

On the way to my apartment, I called Thomas to see if I could stop by. I went into his home and I saw a letter was on the countertop. I picked up and it was Kevin's writing. I had a suspicious thought. What kind of man sent a letter to Thomas? Was there something I did not know about? Was it a set-up? Did both of them plan something when I was in the crazy hospital? In the letter, I saw Kevin's home in California. I did not say anything to Thomas about the letter and I was sat on the floor for about 30 minutes and got out of his home. I stopped at Thomas' because I had guidance. I did not know what that meant but I knew that someday I would find the truth. I was getting better at analyzing my dreams and searching for the truth, and about why things had happened; I needed to know on a deeper level why I was dropped on the Earth. I needed to find my purpose. I couldn't shake off seeing Kevin's letter.

Twenty-One

It was March of 1997 and I had been living in my apartment for two years. I got a note from the landlord that they would be raising the rent. I thought I needed to manage my money better instead of throwing it away. It seemed to me I worked harder than a lot of people but I wasn't gaining anything. I was tired of living day by day without promise of my future and an enormous pressure rose inside of me. I felt that the pressure would burst and would hurt me more than anything that I had ever experienced in life. Suddenly, I saw my life had given me never-ending struggles, and I wanted to make it better. I was actually gaining self-realization of who I was, and hoped that someday my struggles would end if I promised myself that I would be here to see how it came out. I had a mission and that was rising above all obstacles in my life.

The first critical decision was getting out my apartment. It would be hard because most house payments would be more than what I was paying in rent. I also had a lot of credit card debt. I did not think about buying a house and I had no idea about a mortgage loan. I was thinking all night long about getting a home, but how?

The next morning, like any other morning, I went to work in the designer's home. I was discussing my rent with my client and how the cost of living was going up all the time. I wanted to buy a home but I did not know where, and told her that I wanted to have freedom. My apartment gave me the security I needed, but I did not have freedom. Besides, I could not play music because people from upstairs came down knocking on my door for me to shut off the stereo. I craved for the freedom that I deserved. I wanted to move somewhere with no one telling me what to do.

It was afternoon; I was throwing away garbage, and I saw the newspaper. I picked it up and saw an advertisement about a mobile home with "No down payment." I called the sales office and the salesperson told me that I must have $1,000 for a down payment. I was nervous about owning a home. It was fabulous news that I would able to have a place called my home. The salesperson told me to meet him the next day. We met at the place and he showed me two different units. I liked the small home with the huge land. I could have a garden. I talked to a couple of my clients and asked them for early payment for my house's down payment. There were two clients who came over to look my mobile home and they said it was a good one. I did not know mobile homes had a stigma. The mortgage company approved me for 12% of financing the house and the term of 15 years. Then, I had rent space for $280 a month for a year. It was a special promotion and in the meantime I could save some money even if the landowner raised the price. It was a better deal than living in an apartment. It was a great reason to buy the place.

At beginning of March I was approved from the mobile home subdivision. I kept calling them about when I could move in but they always had some kind of excuse. The time was running out from my apartment and I was become anxious about loosing $1,000. I called the mobile home manager at the office and asked them, "Are you discriminating against me because I am Korean?" The next day, someone from the Mobile Home Park called me saying I could move in on the 30th. I had been discriminated against for a month but what did I know about discrimination? This home had been empty for a while, and I bought it at a reasonable cost, I thought. Then, I called my ex-husband and told him that I was moving. I asked him if he could give me two month's alimony and if he could drive a moving truck. He agreed to help me settle in my home. Thomas and his girlfriend came and helped me move everything from my apartment to Macomb, Michigan.

I've moved far away from a major city. One of my client's husbands came over also to help Thomas. It took all day to move and Thomas did a lot of work. I was thankful because Thomas was still showing his friendship. In the late afternoon, Thomas paid me off at once all my alimony that he had owed, plus $1,000 more. I thanked him. I took it as an extra gift from him. *How long had I waited to own a home?* All my life I'd wanted and wished for it and I finally got it. This home was all mine and I worked hard for it. I thought about my home a year before I got divorced. I lived in that home for less than a year with Thomas and I was not happy at all in it. My new home, though a mobile home, made me happy.

I felt an attachment to this home right away and I felt that I had lived here before. I felt that this was my new beginning, and I promised to be strong would make it to the end with my God. Once more, I could trust myself and I would be fine. My faith journey had begun in March 31, 1997. I never thought that I would own a home, car, and I had both in the same year, including being my own boss. I planned what my house would look like. I had a dream of planting a lot of flowers, trees, vegetables and of course, green grass. My driveway was in perfect condition, and the subdivision would lay new grass because one part of the ground was bare. I like this home because the previous owner had built a deck and extended dining room so it looks bigger than any single home.

There was such happiness within me and I could not describe it. I did not feel tired. I kept on working my job during the day, and when I came home I worked a few more hours on my yard. In the spring, I planted wildflowers and made a vegetable garden. In the summer, wildflowers bloomed delightfully through the late fall, and the vegetables I had planted were picked when I needed them: tomatoes, lettuce, eggplant and cucumbers. I have a green thumb and anything I want to grow gives me no trouble at all. I've found the enjoyment of growing plants and touching the earth made me grateful to the Creator. I was content with the simple pleasure of watching my vegetables grow. I never knew farming but I could feel how to be a farmer. I became a more active person than ever before, and I felt that the tremendous amount of comfort, strength and energy flowing through me from somewhere.

In my eyes, there was no need for judgments of the world or the people in it. I discovered that the secrets of life were living inside me and I accepted them unconditionally. The love of God and goodness, kindness was inside of me. I was learning the principles of life. God was sitting in the center of my heart; He knew when I needed something and I was received it like overflowing water. It was an incredible sweetness. I promised Him that I would commit the spiritual part of me to Him first, and put everything earthly second.

I had been lived in this home for couple of months and everything had been settled. I had a small gathering for a house warming party. I invited my neighbors and Thomas' family, his mom, Thomas and Trish for dinner. Then in late summer Thomas sent me a wedding invitation; he and Trish were getting married. I realized that was reason he paid me my alimony at once. I did not go his wedding but I sent him wedding picture frame, and for their happiness. At that point I felt that Thomas had not thought about how I would feel. I sensed that she had been pregnant I knew they would had wedding but sending an invitation was little extreme, I thought. I like both of them but there were difference between ways I accept things as a friend. Thomas did not think. After they got married, they had a baby girl, and since then, I had not seen them for many years but Trish had been sending me a Christmas card every year and I sent her one also. I wished them a good life and happiness. I did not have a husband but I was happy without one.

I was exhausted from too many hours of work. I was stressed

about the high demands of my profession. It was about the middle of April 1997; I laid down on the couch for awhile before I went to work. I was so tired that morning, my front door was open and I fell asleep. *I had a dream of my mom and dad. Mom was wearing a white dress and she had a smile on her face. I never saw her smile while she was on earth. My father was standing next to her. He was reaching his hands out to my mother. I saw both of them together for the first time. It was nice to see them reconciled.* I woke up from the dream and was ready for work. I went out and noticed that there was a pair of doves sitting on the hood of my car. The pair of doves was white and I had never seen them before. I felt that I wanted to touch them and talk with them like I was talking to a person. The doves did not fly away for awhile. They hung around under my Jeep. I waited a few minutes for them to fly away. In the meantime, I made myself a cup of coffee. I was still watching the creatures that belonged to God, and I was beginning to appreciate the beauties of the spiritual world. I grasped the meaningfulness of my life. I thought that the things happening in my life were happening for a reason.

I had to go to work. As I opened the front door, the pair of doves made an appearance from under the hood. The birds ran like the wind then spread their beautiful white wings and took off from my driveway. They circled around in the air in front of my driveway then flew away toward the northwest sky. I felt that doves left me some kind of a message. I had never seen white doves and from that day on. I began to settle down a little better. I wasn't jumpy anymore, not like before. I was less worried about my life.

I understood that God was here to help me and guide me. I asked God to be always on my side; I promised to always have a connection with Him through my prayers and dreams. In order to become a better human being, God was the only source that I could trust. I had to know how to listen and I had to act on it. Through trust in God, I had to fulfill my purpose. In this way, I could help a lot of people. I thought that in this world, there were people like me, but they should never live the life that I had lived. There shouldn't be any more victims but only the winners, striving for happiness in human life. There should be no more tears in human life, and no more sadness in everyone's heart. I declared that I would no longer be a victim. Manifestations of insight and healing of my inner child came with time; I recognized a little girl who had an unbearably harsh life and felt she didn't belong anywhere on earth. I felt that I had died without knowing the sunlight, that I was a beautiful blossoming tree that never had a chance to grow into its purpose. I was wildflowers and I was all four seasons of the earth in human form.

I was living in two different cultures, Korean, and American. The personal revelation of the past was imprinted on my heart, yet I knew I had to rise from it, no matter how difficult that might be. I now know I am the one in charge of my life and this is the reason I came to the United States. I will be living many more years to comprehend this life and I will have the answers for all of it someday. Now I realize that before I was conceived in my mother's womb, there was my destiny. I am still growing and expanding my horizons. This is the first part of my journey, and now I have a chance to soar and reach the sky.